Welcome

Dear students and instructors,

Thank you for choosing Instrument Helicopter Study Notes for your studying needs. We are sure you will find the book very helpful!

If you need additional help, please consult your Certified Flight Instructor Instrument. This book is intended for study use only and is not an official source of teaching/instructing material.

The majority of material covered in this book is a collection of notes gathered throughout years from publications, free and/or paid.

FlyAway Apps, LLC

Copyright

Acknowledgements

**PTS - U.S. Department of Transportation Instrument Helicopter **PTS FAA-S-8081-4E

**HFH - Helicopter Flying Handbook, FAA-H-8083-21A

**PPG - Sanderson. (2007). Private pilot: guided flight discovery. Englewood, CO: Jeppesen Sanderson.

**POH - Robinson Helicopters R22 Beta II Pilot Operating Handbook

FAR/AIM - FAR/AIM Aviation Regulations 2015

**IFH - Instrument Flying Handbook FAA-H-8083-15B

**PMIF - The Pilot's Manual Instrument Flying (5th ed.). (2006). Newcastle, Wash.: Aviation Supplies & Academics.

<u>**Attitude Instruments & Flying**</u>

3 Fundamentals of Instrument Flying **PMIF

✦(CIA)

✦Cross Check

✦Interpretation of Instruments

✦Aircraft Control

*INSTRUMENT SCANNING TECHNIQUES **PMIF*

Cross Check

✦Scanning the Instruments in a specific pattern.
- *L Scan + 1*
- *BAR Scan + 1*

✦(If AI is INOP)
- *Inverted V Scan +1*

✦(If HI + AI are INOP)

✦**Each scan gives us the most information with the least amount of eye movement for our specific instrument panel layout. Less eye movement minimizes fatigue.

Scanning Errors

✦Fixation

✦Omission

✦Emphasis (More importance on one than another)

✦Note: Always cover INOP instruments to prevent looking at them.

Interpretation of Instruments

✦Interpreting the readings of each instrument.

Aircraft Control – Two Methods.

✦Control and Perform Method (method we use)
- *Set the control instruments to a known value to achieve desired results. (Use the maneuvers guide to establish our "known values")*
- *Control Instruments*
  - Control aircraft movements.
    - Attitude Indicator – Pitch, Bank
    - Manifold Pressure – Power setting
    - Tachometer – Verify RPM output
  - Performance Instruments – Displays how aircraft is performing with the control settings.
  - All remaining instruments other than control instruments.

- Emphasis: Using control instruments to set up the maneuver, then monitoring "performance (i.e. "L-Scan")" for necessary adjustments.

✦**Primary and Supporting Method**

- *For every flight maneuver there is a primary and supporting instrument for bank, pitch and power.*
  - These instruments differ for each maneuver.

Required IFR Instruments (**FAR 91.205)

✦Includes ALL VFR instruments + GGGICARA

✦Gyro- AI

✦Gyro- HI

✦Gyro- TC

✦Inclinometer (shows quality of turn)

✦Clock- w/ timer (Hrs. + min. + sec.)

✦Altimeter- pressure sensitive (adjustable)

✦Radio (2-way) and Navigation equipment suitable for route flown.

- *Note: VOR (civilian) or TACAN (military) or an Operable + Suitable RNAV system is required within Class B airspace.*

✦Alternator or generator

*GYROSCOPIC PRINCIPLES **PMIF*

Rigidity in Space

✦Once spinning, a gyro tends to remain in a fixed position and resist other external forces. (tire and string)

Gyroscopic Precession

✦A force applied to a gyro takes affect 90° later in the direction of the turn. (pen and CD)

✦Two ways Gyros are spun up::

- *Vacuum -*
  - high speed air drawn into instrument case, spinning the gyros, powered by engine driven suction pump
    - Pros: Reliable
    - Cons: Heavy
- *Electric*
  - Pros: Lighter
  - Cons: Can fail easily

✦NOTE: Gyros can either be vacuum or electric. *R-22 gyros are all electric for weight purposes and thus are subject to power and/or electrical failures. Vacuum systems work by an engine driven pump sucking air through he instruments and spinning it.

✦NOTE: IFR requires both vacuum and electric for gyros for redundancy.

*ATTITUDE INDICATOR (AI) **PMIF*

✦Provides a direct and immediate picture of pitch and bank.

How it Works

✦"Rigidity in Space"

✦Horizontal gyro (spins parallel to horizon line) with a vertical axis. (Gives us the correct display)

✦Gyro remains in a fixed position relative to the horizon as a/c rotates around it.

- *Two Gimbals one to allow pitch and one to allow roll.*
- *A gimbal is a pivot point that allows the instrument housing to spin around the gyro allowing the gyro to remain in a fixed position.*

Display Components

✦Artificial Horizon

✦Miniature Airplane

✦Bank Index

- *Markings at 10°, 20°, 30°, 60° + 90°*

✦-Pitch Index + Bar

- *White horizontal bars*

Standard Rate Turns

✦360 º turn in 2 min

✦Bank Angle for

- *=A/S÷10 = ans. + 1/2 ans.*
  - *e.g 80 Knots: 80 ÷ 10 = 8 + 4 = 12°*
- **Roll out of turn at half the bank angle.....For 80 kts, roll out 6° prior. (12°÷2=6°)*

Associated Errors

✦Power Failure (Flag Drop)

- *Horizon may fall to one side*

✦Precession Error

- *While turning the AI will show a slight turn in opposite direction, less than 5°, with the greatest error turning through the 180° part of the turn.*
- *A 360° turn will cancel this error.*

✦Tumble Error

- *Extreme attitudes of 60-70° pitch or 100-110° banking roll, gyro may tumble.*

✦Acceleration Error

- *Indicates nose high. (Demonstrate with water bottle)*

✦Deceleration Error

- *Indicates nose low. (Demonstrate with water bottle)*

Preflight Checks
✦Self erected in 5 minutes or less. (Remember to start the clock on start-up)

✦Horizon is level.

✦No power flag.

✦No more than 5° bank when turning.

*HEADING INDICATOR (HI) **PMIF*
✦Used because a magnetic compass only works accurately in straight and level unaccelerated flight.

✦More accurate than the compass.

How it Works
✦"Rigidity in Space"

  • *Vertical gyro with a horizontal axis.*

✦Slave or free mode.

  • *In slave mode, slave unit compensates for drift.*

  • *In free mode, HI must be adjusted every 15 min. in S+L flight.*

✦Has precession error causing drift - acceptable up to 3 ° in 15 minutes

  • *In slave mode, use 3° deviation as a rule of thumb to decide when to use free mode or whether to note error and continue in slave mode. If continuous drifting occurs in slave mode, the instrument is erroneous or broken.*

  • ***In free mode, HI should not deviate more than 3° in 15 min. If this occurs, placard INOP and change scan.*

Display
✦Circular compass card

  • *Display*

  • *Automatically rotates*

    • Airplane always facing direction magnetic heading

    • Usually a heading bug

    • Tick marks

  • *Located every 5° to reduce mental math*

Associated Errors
✦Power Failure

  • *Heading flag drops to give indication. If no flag, power failure is typically confirmed when drift is more than 3° in 15 min or less.*

  • *Heading Flag*

✦Drift

- *HI gradually drifts off the correct magnetic direction because of internal mechanical reasons such as friction and gimbal affect and not to mention apparent drift. (ONLY occurs in free mode unless instrument is broken.)*
  - *Nav Flag*
- ✦Apparent Drift
  - *Results from the earth's rotation. As the earth rotates about its axis at 15 per hour, the direction in space from a point on the earth's surface to north continually changes.*
- ✦Ticking
  - *Gyro failure or vacuum problem*
- ✦Sliding
  - *More or less than normal - Flux valve error*

Other types
- ✦Directional Gyro - Looks like mag. compass. Compass heading stay inline with mag. N.
- ✦Remote Indicating Compass - HI + Flux valve & slave mode
- ✦HSI

*HORIZONTAL SITUATION INDICATOR (HSI) **PMIF*
- ✦Combines HI & CDI (Course & Deviation Indicator)
- ✦HI is super imposed w/ navigation information
- ✦Gives VOR or Localizer info. (Horizontal Guidance)
- ✦Glide Slope indicator. (Vertical Guidance)

How it Works
- ✦"Rigidity in Space"
- ✦Vertical gyro with a horizontal axis.

Display
- ✦Airplane
- ✦Tick-marks
  - *Every 5° of compass rose*
  - *Actual heading marker*
  - *Level*
  - *Standard Rate Turn*
- ✦OBS (Omni-Bearing Selector)
- ✦CDI (Course Deviation Indicator)
- ✦Glide slope markings
- ✦Heading Bug with selector knob

5 Components
- ✦Flux Valve

- *Senses magnetic north and is located under the pilot side floor board.*
- ✦Slave Unit
  - *Selector switch next to cyclic for slave or free mode. (Aligns card with north with help of the slave unit. Much like our gov. helps with our RPM's)*
- ✦Gyro
  - *Under the passenger seat.*
- ✦Display
  - *Located on the instrument panel.*
- ✦VHF Radio Navigation
  - *Navigation frequency selector located in GPS. (A popular receiver is the Garmin 430 which uses both VHF and satellites)*

Preflight
- ✦Check heading with MC in slave mode.
- ✦No power flag.
- ✦If more than 3° deviation, not error or set to free mode and align with MC.

TURN COORDINATOR AND TURN INDICATOR (TC, TI) **PMIF
- ✦TI- Older model
  - *Rate of turn (degree of bank)*
  - *No roll indication*
- ✦TC- Newer model
  - *Canted 30° to get two additional inputs*
  - *Direction (Yaw)*
  - *Rate of turn (degree of bank)*
  - *Rate of roll*

How it Works
- ✦"Gyroscopic Precession"
- ✦Vertical gyro with a horizontal axis. (Instrument p. 50+51)

Display Components
- ✦Airplane
- ✦Tick marks
  - *Level*
  - *Standard rate*

Limitations
- ✦Gives no indication of pitch
- ✦Power failure

Preflight Checks
✦Wings level.
✦No power flag. (Hdg. Flag is the power flag)
✦Wings tilt when yawing.

*INCLINOMETER/COORDINATION BALL **PMIF*
✦Shows quality of turn
  • *Slip or skid*
✦No power source.
✦Step on the ball to stay in trim.
  • *(If ball is to the right, add right pedal for proper trim and vice versa)*

Preflight
✦Full of fluid.
✦No bubbles or cracks.
✦Ball at the bottom/center.
✦Note when hovering where ball is located. (Only way to know when in trim)

*MAGNETIC COMPASS (MC) **PMIF*

✦No power source.

Common Errors
✦(VDMONA)
✦Variation
  • *Due to magnetic declination.*
✦Deviation
  • *Due to other magnetic forces inside A/C.*
✦Magnetic dip
  • *(Half the Latitude + Bank Angle)(Closer to poles = pulls compass down, unleveled)*
✦Oscillation
  • *Fluid dampens the movement of the compass*
✦Northern turning error
  • *UNOS*
    • Undershoot North by 25° by rolling out early
    • Overshoot South by 15° by rolling out late
✦Acceleration
  • *ANDS*
    • Acceleration North
    • Deceleration South

- *On E or W heading, compass points north when accelerating and south when decelerating.*
- *Due to the weight added for mag. dip error*

Preflight

✦Full of fluid.

✦No cracks or bubbles.

✦Level.

✦Deviation card in place.

CLOCK OR TIMER

✦Must have hours, minutes and seconds.

OTHER INSTRUMENTS **PMIF

✦Tachometer

✦Temperatures

✦Oil Pressure

✦Carb.Heat

✦Every additional gauge in aircraft

Power Indicators

✦Manifold Pressure Gauge (MAP)

✦Tachometer

- *Engine RPM sensor is driven by right magneto.*
- *Rotor RPM sensor is located forward of the flex coupling/yoke flange assembly.*
- *(2 magnetic sensors on drive shaft)*

PITOT-STATIC SYSTEM **PMIF

✦Airspeed Indicator (ASI)

- *Must be check within preceding 24 calendar months ****FAR 91.411*

✦Vertical Speed Indicator (VSI)

- *No required inspection*

✦Altimeter (Alt)

- *Must be check within preceding 24 calendar months ****FAR 91.411*

AIRSPEED INDICATOR (ASI) **PMIF

✦Displays your Indicated airspeed.

How it Works

✦Uses ram air pressure.

- *Airspeed increases, pressure decreases and conversely.*

✦Connected to the pitot tube.

✦Contains a diaphragm.

• *Expands and contracts with pressure*

Preflight Checks

✦Confirm that a speed is indicated when in forward motion.

✦Pitot tube and static port are clear.

• *Types of Airspeed*

• Indicated Airspeed (IAS)-

• The speed indicated on the ASI.

• Calibrated Airspeed (CAS)-

• The airspeed calibrated at higher speeds due to the angle of the pitot tube.

• True Airspeed (TAS)-

• The speed that the aircraft is traveling. Can be higher than IAS due to higher altitudes and less dense air moving through the pitot.

• Ground Speed (GS)-

• The speed of the aircraft across the ground.

*VERTICAL SPEED INDICATOR (VSI) **PMIF*

✦Readout of the rate of change in altitude, ascending or descending.

How it Works

✦Measures the difference in air pressure.

✦Measured in feet per minute up to 2000'

✦Metered leak inside instrument casing. (Causing a trend)

✦Expandable capsule.

Limitations

✦Trend Instrument.

✦6 to 9 second delay.

✦Bounces in rough flight

✦Blockage. (Inoperable)

Preflight Checks

✦Indicates zero.

✦If not indicating zero, note its measurement and use as new absolute zero.

✦May be adjusted to zero if applicable. (Consult mechanic)

*ALTIMETER (ALT) **PMIF*

How it Works

✦Sealed Capsule.

✦Aneroid Wafer. (Contains fixed amount of air. 29.92")
✦Pressure Window.   (Kollsman Window)
✦Allows for adjusting to local pressure setting.

Preflight Checks

✦Static port is clear.
✦Indicates altitude within 75' of airport elevation.

Instrument Flying Maneuvers

STRAIGHT AND LEVEL FLIGHT

- ✦See your school's maneuvers guide

Common Errors

- ✦Improper pitch
- ✦Not maintaining altitude
- ✦Not scanning properly
- ✦Improper power settings
- ✦Drifting off heading
- ✦Not maintaining proper trim
- ✦Over-controlling pitch and bank during corrections
- ✦Failure to maintain desired airspeed

LEVEL TURNS

- ✦See your school's maneuvers guide

Common Errors

- ✦Not maintaining proper bank angle
- ✦Not maintaining altitude (Not lateral ONLY cyclic)
- ✦Not scanning properly
- ✦Not rolling out appropriately (Not calculating)
- ✦Failure to maintain trim

STEEP TURNS

- ✦See your school's maneuvers guide

Common Errors

- ✦Not maintaining proper bank angle (Always 30°)
- ✦Not maintaining altitude (Loss of vertical lift, so add ~1" of MAP)
- ✦Not scanning properly
- ✦Not rolling out appropriately (Always 15° prior regardless of A/S)
- ✦Failure to maintain trim

CONSTANT AIRSPEED CLIMBS

- ✦See your school's maneuvers guide
- ✦Begin level off at 10% of the vertical speed

Common Errors

- ✦Not maintaining A/S

◆Drifting of heading

◆Improper use of power

◆Poor control of pitch attitude

◆Failure to maintain proper trim

◆Not leveling off on desired altitude (<100' use cyclic, >100' use coll.)

CONSTANT AIRSPEED DESCENTS

◆See your school's maneuvers guide

◆Begin level off at 10% of the vertical speed

Common Errors

◆Not maintaining A/S

◆Drifting of heading

◆Improper use of power

◆Poor control of pitch attitude

◆Failure to maintain proper trim

◆Not leveling off on desired altitude (<100' use cyclic, >100' use coll.)

CONSTANT RATE CLIMBS

◆See your school's maneuvers guide

◆Begin level off at 10% of the vertical speed

Common Errors

◆Not maintaining constant rate of climb

◆Drifting of heading

◆Improper use of power

◆Poor control of pitch attitude

◆Failure to maintain proper trim

◆Not leveling off on desired altitude (<100' use cyclic, >100' use coll.)

CONSTANT RATE DESCENTS

◆See your school's maneuvers guide

◆Begin level off at 10% of the vertical speed

Common Errors

◆Not maintaining constant rate of climb

◆Drifting of heading

◆Improper use of power

◆Poor control of pitch attitude

◆Failure to maintain proper trim

✦Not leveling off on desired altitude (<100' use cyclic, >100' use coll.)

CLIMBING AND DESCENDING TURNS

✦See your school's maneuvers guide

Common Errors

✦Not maintaining proper bank angle

✦Not rolling out appropriately

✦Not leveling off at desired altitude

✦Not maintaining appropriate climb, or descent (In constant rate)

✦Failure to maintain desired airspeed (In constant airspeed)

✦Improper use of power

✦Failure to maintain trim

UNUSUAL ATTITUDE RECOVERY

✦See your school's maneuvers guide

✦Bank, Pitch, Power

Common Errors

✦Not correcting in BPP (Bank, Pitch, Power) order

✦Not resuming prior flight configuration

✦Recovering too abruptly (Nose high could lead to low g)

Common Errors Leading to Unusual Attitude:

✦Not maintaining proper trim

✦Poor CRM

✦Improper scanning (e.g.. Fixation)

✦Attempting to recover from sensory sensations other than sight

✦Failure to practice basic attitude instrument flying (CIA)

PARTIAL PANEL FLYING

✦Loss of Instrument reliability and confirmed failure

✦Change of scan and increased awareness

✦Notify ATC of any failures and state:

- Who you are
- What broke (GGGICARA)
- Your capabilities to continue flight
- Any help needed

• *A VSI outage may be an example of when you may NOT contact ATC but whenever it doubt, contact.*

✦If AI fails:
- *Vacuum failure or electrical failure (GGGICARA)*
- *Usually shows a climbing left or right turn*
- *Detected by scanning other instruments*

✦Rely on TC for bank and VSI for pitch (Bar scan +1)

✦If HI fails:
- *Will not show correct heading and not turn when aircraft turns*
- *HDG flag or drifting off course*
- *Notify ATC*
- *Rely on TC for bank*
- *Use compass turns and timed turns*
- *Inverted v-scan*

Pitot Static System Failures

Situation	Airspeed	Altimeter	VSI
1. Blocked pitot	Zero	Works	Works
2. Blocked pitot and drain hole. Open static	High in climb Low in descent (like an altimeter)	Works	Works
3. Blocked static-open pitot	Low in climb High in descent	Frozen	Frozen
4. Using alternate cockpit static air	Reads high	Reads high	Momentarily shows a climb
5. Broken VSI glass	Reads high	Reads high	reverses

TIMED TURNS

✦See your school's maneuvers guide

Common Errors

✦Not starting timer after turn

✦Not watching the timer and anticipating rollout

✦Compass chasing (Do not look at compass for a few seconds after rollout to prevent chasing)

COMPASS TURNS

✦UNOS(Undershoot North, Overshoot South)

- *Turns into the north lag*
- *Turns into the south lead*

Common Errors

✦Not compensating for turning errors

Meteorology

The Atmosphere (**PPG 6-2)
✦Consists of Three layers
- *Troposphere (Greek for "turn" or "change")*
  - Surface to 36,000' (estimate)
  - Most weather occurs
  - Composition
    - 78% nitrogen
    - 21% oxygen
    - 1% argon/ carbon dioxide
    - 1-4% water vapor
- *Tropopause*
  - Lid to troposphere
- *Stratosphere*
  - 36,000 – 160,000'
  - Same as troposphere but less dense

Atmospheric Circulation ****PPG
✦Movement of air relative to earths surface
✦Convection
- *The circulation of warm air rising and cold air falling, warm air rising from equator toward poles and conversely*
- *Convection (result of uneven heating of earth) **PPG 6-5*
  - Heated air
    - Molecules spread apart
    - Less dense air
  - Cooler air
    - Molecules pack together
    - More dense air
  - Result = cool/ heavier air replaces warm/ lighter weight rising air
- *Convection and atmospheric circulation (**PPG 6-6)*
  - Solar energy strikes equator at higher concentration than poles
  - Cooler air at poles sinks and flows towards rising and warmer air at equator
- *Atmospheric pressure*
- *Low pressure areas*
  - Warmer, less dense air
- *High pressure areas*

- Cooler more dense air
  - Result
    - Air moves from cool dense areas of high pressure to warmer less dense areas of low pressure
- *Atmospheric pressure and circulation (**PPG 6-7)*
  - Pressure gradient – change of pressure over distance
  - Isobars – areas of equal pressure
    - Isobars spread wide = weak pressure gradient
    - Isobars close together = strong pressure gradient
    - Isobars help identify high and low pressure systems (**PPG 6-7)
    - Strong winds result w/ strong pressure gradient
- ✦Coriolis force (**PPG 6-9)
  - *Earths rotation causes all weather to follow curved path*
  - *Air follows isobars*
  - *Air flows to right in northern hemisphere*
  - *Characteristics of high/ low pressure systems (**PPG 6-9)*
    - High pressure system
      - Air flows out and clockwise (draw picture)
    - Low pressure systems
      - Air flows up and counterclockwise (draw picture)

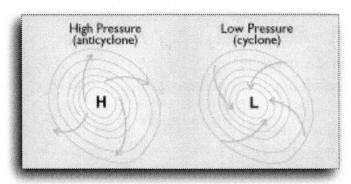

- *Surface friction (**PPG 6-9)*
  - Earths surface slows moving air
  - Affects air within 2000' of earths surface

Moisture

- ✦Three physical states
  - *Solid, Liquid, Gas*
- ✦Changes of states (**PPG 6-19)
  - *Evaporation – liquid to vapor*
  - *Condensation – water vapor to liquid*

- *Sublimation – frozen state to water vapor*
- *Deposition – water vapor to ice*
- *Melting – frozen state to liquid*
- *Freezing – liquid to frozen*

✦Relative humidity
- *Actual amount of moisture present compared to how much could be*
- *Influenced by higher temp.*
- *Hotter air: less dense, more room for water vapor*
- *Cooler air: more dense, less room for water vapor*

✦Dew point
- *Point at which air must be cooled to no longer hold water*
- *Point where air is supporting 100% of moisture it can hold*
- *Temp/ dew point spread (**PPG 6-20)*
- *when equal relative humidity = 100%*
- *small spread = visible atmospheric moisture*

WEATHER PATTERNS (**PPG 6-16)

Atmospheric Stability
✦Stability – resistance to vertical motion
✦Stable vs. unstable \
- *Stable (PVCTIP)*
  - Pressure System - High
  - Visibility - poor
  - Clouds - stratus
  - Turbulence - none, smooth
  - Ice - rime
  - Precipitation - steady, can last for days
- *Unstable*
  - Pressure System - Low
  - Visibility - good
  - Clouds - cumulus
  - Turbulence - more severe
  - Ice - clear ice
  - Precipitation - Fast/ Showery/ T-Storms

✦Adiabatic cooling/ heating
- *Rising air expands from lower atmospheric pressure at altitude*
- *Air moving downward is compressed by higher pressure at lower altitudes*

✦Heating/ cooling

- *Temp. change of dry air due to compression(warms)/ expansion(cools)*

✦Standard lapse rate
- *Rate at which temp. decreases w/ altitude*
- *2 degrees C per 1000'*

✦Temp. inversions
- *Cooler air trapped/ located below warmer air*
- *Smooth, stable layer of air*
- *Restricted visibility below inversion*
- *Turbulence above inversion*
- *2 types*
  - Surface based temp. inversion
    - Cool/ clear/ calm nights
    - Ground cools lowers temp. of air
    - Frontal temp. inversions
    - Cool air forced under warm air
    - Warm air spreads over cooler air

Clouds (**PPG 6-21)
✦Cloud Composition (Formation)
- *Moist air cooled to its dew point*
- *Small temp./ dew point spread (2 degrees C)*
- *Condensation nuclei*

✦Four families of clouds
- *Low clouds*
  - SFC to 6,500' AGL
  - Composed of super cool water drops
  - Stratus "Layer", nimbo-(prefix or suffix meaning "rainclouds") stratus, stratocumulus
  - Rime ice
- *Middle clouds*
  - 6,500 – 20,000'
  - Composed of large super cool water drops
  - Alto, Altostratus, altocumulus
  - Mixed ice
- *High clouds*
  - 20,000' – 60,000'
  - Composed of ice particles
  - Cirrus "ringlet" or "wispy", cirrocumulus, cirrostratus
  - No icing

- *Extensive vertical development*
  - Any altitude
  - Composed of all
  - Very unstable/ turbulent
  - Cumulus (suffix meaning "heap" or "puffy"), cumulonimbus, towering cumulus
  - All types of ice and hail

Air Masses (**PPG 6-28)

✦Definition
  - *Large parcel of air w/ uniform: temp. & moisture*

✦Airmass classification
  - *Polar/ tropical*
    - Polar = cooler climate
    - Tropical = warmer climate
  - *Continental/ maritime*
    - Continental = dry
    - Maritime = moist

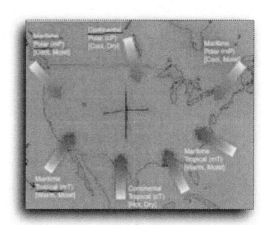

✦Fronts (**PPG 6-32)
  - *Boundaries between air-masses creates hazards to flying*
  - *Cold front*
    - Cold air displacing warm air
    - Cold, dense, stable air moves along sfc. and shovels up warm air
    - Fast moving and turbulent
    - Worse wx to come
    - Commonly associated w/
      - Temp. inversions
      - Cumulus clouds
      - T- storms
      - Sporadic storms
  - *Warm fronts*
    - warm air overtaking & displacing cold air
    - Warm air slides over cool air
    - Slow moving
    - Better wx
    - Commonly associated w/
      - Steady rain
      - Smooth air
      - Temp. inversions

- *Stationary fronts – collision of two air masses w/ similar characteristics*
  - Remain stationary
  - Common associated w/
    - Mix between cold and warm front
- *Occluded front – fast moving cold front catches slower moving warm front*
  - Cold front occlusion
    - Cold front is slower than the slow moving warm front
    - Cold air slide under warmer air forcing warm front aloft
  - Warm front occlusion
    - Air ahead of slow moving warm front is colder than that w/ in the fast moving cold front
    - Cold front rides up over the warm front and forces cold front aloft

WEATHER HAZARDS (**PPG 6-39)

Thunderstorms
- ✦Single greatest threat to aviation
- ✦Conditions Necessary for Formation
  - *High moisture content*
  - *Unstable air*
  - *Uplifting force*
- ✦Life cycle of t-storm (Three Stages)
  - *Cumulus stage*
  - *Building of clouds*
    - Average 15 minutes
    - Updrafts
  - *Mature stage*
    - Precipitation
    - 15- 30 minutes
    - Updrafts/ downdrafts
    - Lightning
    - Anvil top to clouds
  - *Dissipating stage*
    - No more precip.
    - Last about 15 minutes
    - Downdrafts
    - Storm goes away
- ✦Squall line thunderstorms
  - *Found ahead of fast moving cold fronts*

- *T- storms in a row*
- *Embedded and hidden*
- *Most dangerous, up to 700 miles wide, high winds, hail and tornadoes*

✦Microbursts (**PPG 6-51) **AIM 832/ 836

- *Most dangerous type of wind shear*
- *Less than 1 NM wide and 1000' tall*
- *Seldom last longer than 15 minutes*
- *100 KT winds possible*
- *6,000 FPM downdrafts*
- *Dangerous when encountered near ground*

✦Virga **PPG 6-27

- *Tiny rain drops that fall and evaporate before reaching ground*
- *Evaporation cools air*
- *Cool air sinks fast*
- *Heavy downdrafts up to 6000' per minute*

✦Thunderstorm avoidance

- *20 NM minimum distance*
- *Turbulence and hail can extend 20 nm*

Turbulence (**PPG 6-44)

✦Wind shear

- *sudden drastic change in wind speed and/ or direction*
- *May occur at any altitude*
- *Vertical/ horizontal*

✦Clear air turbulence

- *Usually occurs around jet stream at altitudes above 15,000'*

✦Wake turbulence

- *see also Ground Lesson #3*
- *Rapid whirl pools of wingtip vortices created from airfoils producing lift*

✦Mechanical turbulence (**PPG 6-64)

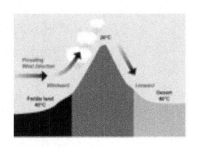

- *Occurs around when obstacles (buildings, terrain) interfering w/ wind flow*
- *Leeward side of object*

Low Visibility

✦Fog (surap)

- *Steam – cold dry air moves above warmer water*
  - *Warm water evaporates and rises, cooled to dew point and condenses*

- (warm pool in winter)
- *Upslope – moist, stable air is forced up sloping land to cooler temp. at higher altitudes*
  - Need at least 15 Kt wind or greater
- *Radiation – calm humid nights*
  - Ground cools
  - Air next to ground cooled to dew point
  - Low lying fog (in valleys where H20 is abundant)
- *Advection – warm/ moist air blown inland over cooler surface*
  - Cool sfc cools air to dew point
  - Need at least 15 Kt wind or greater
- *Precipitation – warm rain falling through cool air*
  - Rain evaporates and cooled to dew point

Icing

- ✦Icing concerns for helicopters
  - *Increased weight and drag*
  - *Unbalanced rotor disc*
  - *Ice shedding into tail rotor*
  - *Covering windscreen*
  - *Blocking pitot tube*
- ✦Structural icing – ice buildup on a/ c surface
  - *Requirements for formation*
  - *Visible moisture*
  - *Surface of a/ c 0 degrees C or colder*
  - *Kinds of structural icing:*
    - Rime ice – (-15 to -20 degrees)
      - Forms in stratus clouds
      - Super cooled small H20 droplets which change structure of airfoil (distorts airfoil)
      - Opaque in color
      - Freezes instantly trapping air
      - Cloudy rough buildup on rotor blade tips
    - Clear ice – 0 to 10 degrees
      - Forms in Cumulus clouds
      - Super cooled large H20 droplets which adhere tenaciously
      - Clear in color
      - Difficult to remove
      - Adds weight and shedding
    - Mixed ice (-10 – (-15) degrees)

- Combo of rime and clear ice
- Cumulus and/ or stratus clouds
- Frost
    - Disrupts smooth airflow
    - Surface must be below freezing air condenses on surface

✦Prevention and elimination
- *Once encountered*
- *Look for ice on protrusions of H/ C (skids,lights,trim strings)*
- *Descend into warmer air*
- *Land or turn around*
- *Anti ice*
    - Glycol based solution on a/ c before flight
- *Heated leading edges*
- *Heated pitot tube*
- *Carb heat*
- *De- ice*
    - Chemical that melts ice
- *Inflatable air filled blade liners*

Cold Weather Operations
✦Allow a/ c to warm up
✦Ensure free of ice
✦Prepared for frozen skids upon pickup

Weather Reports & Charts

WEATHER HAZARDS

★Inclement weather can be very dangerous to any aircraft and their occupants

- *Strong winds*
- *Blowing dust*
- *Updrafts and downdrafts*
- *Heavy precipitation*
- *Thunderstorms*
- *Wind shear*

★In weather conditions with low visibility (clouds, fog, haze), it is very difficult for a VFR pilot to maintain control of their aircraft

OBTAINING WEATHER INFORMATION

★Official (recommended) Sources:

- *1-800-WX-BRIEF*
- *WWW.DUATS.COM*
- *These sources are official because your tail number is recorded and documented with the weather briefing.*

★Unofficial Sources:

- *Looking outside*
- *Television (Weather Channel, etc)*
- *Internet sources (weather.com)*
- *Newspaper*

PRINTED WEATHER REPORTS AND FORECASTS

METAR (Aviation Routine Meteorological Report) (**PPG 7-10)

★Reports current surface conditions

- *Updated every hour between 45 minutes past the hour and the hour.*
- *Same format as ATIS report*
    - Type of report (METAR, SPECI)
    - Station ICAO (International Civil Aviation Organization) Identifier (KCHD)
    - Date and Time of Report (301515)
    - Modifier (optional) (AO1, A02)
    - Wind (08020G38KT)

- Visibility (6 SM)
- Runway Visual Range (if required)
- Weather (weather codes: SH, TS, BR)
- Sky condition and clouds
  - Few - 0- 2/8 sky coverage
  - Scattered (SCT) - 3/8 - 4/8 sky coverage
  - Broken (BKN) - 5/8 - 7/8 sky coverage
  - Overcast (OVC) - 8/8 sky coverage
  - Ceiling is the lowest level listed as broken or overcast
- *Temperature/ Dew Point*
- *Altimeter setting*
- *Remarks (RMK...)*

PIREP (Pilot Report) (**PPG7-17)

★Pireps are real-time weather information (actual weather that someone else is flying through).

★Anytime you encounter unforecasted weather you are encouraged to make a pirep.

★File with FSS or EFAS 122.2

★The form to follow when filing a pirep is as follows:

★Mandatory items

- *Type of report (UA, UUA)*
  - UA- routine or UUA urgent
- *OV - Location*
- *TM – Zulu time*
- *FL- Flight Level or Altitude*
- *TP – Aircraft Type*

★Non-mandatory items (only include if in existence)

- *SK – Sky cover*
- *WX – Visibility and Weather*
- *TA – Temperature*
- *WV – Wind*
- *TB – Turbulence*
- *IC – Icing*
- *RM Remarks*

TAF (Terminal Aerodrome Forecast)(**PPG 7-20)(AIM 7-1-30)

★ Issued 4X per day, valid for 24 hours

★ Valid for the reporting airport and up to a 5 statute mile radius circle around that airport.

- *"VC" in report changes reporting radius of 5 to 10 statute mile*

★ Provides FORECAST information in a METAR format.

★ Is a report of FUTURE weather, not current weather.

FA (Area Forecast) (**PPG 7-20)

★ Issued 3X per day

★ Valid for a total of 18 hours (12 hours forecast and a 6 hour categorical outlook)

★ Covers an area the size of several states

★ Six (6) different FA regions in contiguous US: SFO, SLC, CHI, DFW, BOS, MIA

★ Comprised of four sections:

- *Communications and product header section: Issue time and valid time*

- *Synopsis: Gives a brief summary of location and movements of fronts, pressure systems and circulation patterns.*

- *VFR clouds and weather section: 12-hour specific forecast*

  - Breaks weather into smaller geographical areas

  - Describes clouds and weather affecting VFR operations.

- *Outlook – Valid for 6 hours.*

FD (Winds and Temperatures Aloft Forecast)

★ Issued 2 times per day

★ No temperatures for 3,000 foot level or within 2,500 feet of station elevation

★ No winds within 1,500 feet of station elevation

★ 9900 denotes winds that are light and variable (less than 5 knots)

★ 0000 denotes calm winds

★ Winds greater than 99 knots shown as

- *-50 +100 (7713 = 270 @ 113 knots)*

★ Wind directions are true north

★ Temperatures are always negative above 24,000'

SEVERE WEATHER REPORTS AND FORECASTS

AC (Convective Outlook) (**PPG 7-25)

★ National forecast of thunderstorm activity covering two 24 hour periods

★ For areas having the chance of thunderstorms

★ Severe thunderstorm criteria includes:

★ Surface winds of 50 knots or higher

★ Hail ¾ inch or greater

★ Tornados

WW (Severe Weather Watch Bulletin)(**PPG 7-25)

★ Denotes areas of possible severe thunderstorms or tornados.

★ Issued on an unscheduled basis and updated as required.

GRAPHIC WEATHER PRODUCTS

Surface Analysis Chart (**PPG 7-31)

★ Issued every 3 hours

★ Wx valid at time of chart

★ Locates fronts and pressure systems

★ Cover entire U.S.

Weather depiction chart

★ Issued every 3 hours

★ Info derived from METAR

★ Shows areas of IFR, VFR, MVFR

- *IFR ceilings vis. < 1000'/ 3sm*

- *VFR ceilings/ vis. > 3000' agl/ 5sm*

- *MVFR ceilings/ vis 1000'-3000' agl/ 3-5sm*

★ Valid at time of issuance

Radar Summary Chart (**PPG 7-34)

★ Issued every hour 35 min. past the hour

★ Collection of radar wx reports

★ Shows precipitation

★ Indicates

- *Intensity of precipitation*

- *Direction and movement*

- *Speed*

- *Tops and bottoms*

Low Level Significant Weather Prognostic Charts (**PPG 7-37)

★ Issued 4 time per day

★ Valid for 24 hours

★ 12 and 24 hour outlook

★ Forecasts

★ Surface to 24,000'

★ Low visibility and ceiling

★ Turbulence and icing

★ Top boxes = areas of IFR/ MVFR/VFR

★ Bottom boxes = precipitation, t-storms, fronts,pressure systems

WA (AIRMETs)(Airmen Meteorological Report)

★ Warn of weather conditions that are hazardous to small aircraft

★ Issued every 6 hours, valid for 6 hours

★ Three types of AIRMET

- *Tango = turbulence*
  - Moderate turbulence
  - Sustained winds of 30 KTS or greater at surface
- *Sierra = mountain obscuration*
  - CIG less than 1000' vis. less than 3 SM affecting 50% or more of an area
- *Zulu = icing*
  - Moderate icing, freezing levels

WS (SIGMET's) (Significant Meteorological Information)

★ Issued for hazardous non convective weather to all aircraft

★ Issued every 4 hours, valid for 4 hours. (If no significant weather, re-issuance will indicate nothing new to report)

★ Includes following conditions:

- *Severe icing*
- *Severe turbulence*
- *Clear air turbulence*
- *Dust storms and sandstorms lowering visibility to less than 3 miles*

- *Volcanic ash*

WST (CONVECTIVE SIGMET's)

★Issued for hazardous convective weather to all aircraft.

★When needed

★Valid for 2 hours until superseded by next issue.

★Includes the following conditions:

- *Tornados*
- *Line of thunderstorms*
- *Thunderstorms over a wide area*
- *Embedded thunderstorms*
- *Hail greater than or equal to ¾" at the surface*
- *Wind gusts to 50 knots or greater.*

★Consists of either an observation and a forecast or simply a forecast

GO, NO-GO DECISIONS

★With current weather information the PIC can make a decision if the flight can be completed safely.

★Decisions should be made by considering the pilot's comfort level with the conditions, not by some outside forces (boss, passengers, schedule, etc).

★Weather comfort can change as experience level changes.

Robinson Helicopter Weather Related Limitations (**POH 2-15)

★No flight when:

- *Surface winds exceed 25 KTS including gusts*
- *Surface wind gust spreads exceed 15 KTS*
- *Continued moderate, severe or extreme turbulence*

★Unless pilot has:

- *200 or more hours in a helicopter*
- *50 hours in R22*
- *Completed awareness training (SFAR 73)*

★Note: Moderate turbulence is turbulence that causes:

- *Changes in altitude or attitude*
- *Variations in indicated airspeed*
- *Feeling strains on the seatbelts*

• *Adjust forward airspeed to between 60 KTS and 0.7 Vne but no lower than 57 KTS, upon inadvertently encountering turbulence.*

EXAMPLES

METAR's

METAR KBUF 021654Z 17003KT 10SM CLR 07/M01 A2986 RMK AO2 SLP118

METAR KPHX 021651Z 09005KT 10SM FEW200 BKN250 13/01 A2994 RMK AO2 SLP132

METAR KSFO 021656Z 00000KT 8SM OVC009 08/06 A3003 RMK AO2 SLP168 T00780056

PIREP's

PVU UA /OV FFU220015 /TM 1611 /FL085 /TP P28A /SK SCT080 /RM O/MTNS E-SE
PVU UA /OV PVU270004 /TM 1624 /FL065 /TP BE20 /SK OVC065 /IC NEG /RM /TA UNKN BA GOOD
HWD UA /OV OAK120007 /TM 1539 /FL018 /TP BE30 /RM BASE009-TOP018
SJC UA /OV SJC /TM 1608 /FL005 /TP B732 /SK OVC005-TOP014 /RM FAP RWY30L
PRB UA /OV AVE/TM 1630/FL370/TP B737/WV 321024KT/TB SMOOTH/RM AWC-WEBSWA
SJC UA /OV SJC /TM 1652 /FL014 /TP B733 /SK OVC006-TOP014
MRY UA /OV MRY /TM 1656 /FL006 /TP DHC6 /SK OVC006
SFO UA /OV SFO120005/TM 1700/FLUNKN/TP UNKN/SK BASE008-TOP018/RM ZOA CWSU

TAF

KBUF 021723Z 0218/0318 16007KT P6SM BKN150
    FM030000 13010KT P6SM -RA OVC080 WS020/17035KT
    FM030200 10010KT 5SM RA OVC015 WS020/13040KT
    FM030500 09008KT 3SM RA BR OVC007 WS020/13030KT
    FM030700 12005KT 4SM -RA BR OVC007
    FM030900 18005KT 5SM -RA BR OVC010
    FM031200 21014G20KT 6SM -RA BR OVC012
    FM031400 24017G28KT P6SM -SHRA OVC015

AREA FORECAST

FAUS45 KKCI 021145
FA5W
SLCC FA 021145
SYNOPSIS AND VFR CLDS/WX
SYNOPSIS VALID UNTIL 030600
CLDS/WX VALID UNTIL 030000...OTLK VALID 030000-030600
ID MT WY NV UT CO AZ NM

.
SEE AIRMET SIERRA FOR IFR CONDS AND MTN OBSCN.
TS IMPLY SEV OR GTR TURB SEV ICE LLWS AND IFR CONDS.
NON MSL HGTS DENOTED BY AGL OR CIG.

.
SYNOPSIS...ALF...TROF NWRN ND INTO NERN UT. MOD WLY FLOW OVR WY
AND NRN CO AHD OF TROF AND MOD NLY FLOW OVR ID AND WRN MT BEHIND
TROF. 06Z TROF SERN SD INTO NERN UT. MOD NLY FLOW OVR ID WRN MT
AND NRN UT. MOD NWLY FLOW OVR SRN CO AND NRN NM. SFC...LOW SWRN
CO. CDFNT FM LOW SWD INTO SERN NM. CDFNT FM LOW WWD INTO SRN NV.

06Z LOW W CNTRL NM WITH CDFNT S INTO SWRN NM. CDFNT FM LOW W INTO SRN NV.

ID
NRN...SKC. OTLK...VFR.
CNTRL MTNS...SCT060. VIS 3SM BR. 14Z OVC060 TO 080. VIS 3SM BR.
  18Z SKC. OTLK...VFR.
SWRN...SCT050. 18Z SKC. OTLK...VFR.
SERN...SKC. OTLK...VFR.

.
MT
W OF CONTDVD...SKC. OTLK...VFR.
SWRN MTNS...SKC. 15Z SCT070. OTLK...VFR.
ERN SLOPES...SKC. 12Z SCT080. 20Z BKN080 TOP 150. OTLK...VFR.
N CNTRL...BKN090 TOP 160. 14Z OVC070. ISOL -SHSN. OTLK...VFR.
S CNTRL...SCT140. 15Z BKN110 TOP 150. OTLK...VFR.
NERN...OVC050 TOP 160. 18Z BKN070. OTLK...VFR.
SERN...OVC080 TOP 160. ISOL -SHSN. 18Z OVC050. ISOL -SHSN.
  OTLK...MVFR CIG BECMG 04Z VFR.

.
WY
NWRN...SKC. OTLK...VFR.
SWRN...OVC110 TOP 100. 18Z SCT110. OTLK...VFR.
NERN...SKC. 23Z BKN090 TOP 160. OTLK...VFR.
SERN...OVC090 TOP FL180. OCNL -SN. 15Z BKN110. OTLK...VFR.

.
NV
NWRN...SCT CI. OTLK...VFR.
NERN...SKC. OTLK...VFR.
SRN...BKN CI. 21Z SKC. OTLK...VFR.

.
UT
NWRN...SCT CI. 23Z SKC. OTLK...VFR.
NERN...SCT120. OTLK...VFR.
SRN...SKC. OTLK...VFR.

.
CO
MTNS
  NRN...OVC070 TOP FL200. ISOL -SHSN. 18Z OVC100. OTLK...VFR.
  SRN...SCT080. 23Z BKN080 TOP FL180. OTLK...MVFR CIG.
WRN...SKC. 16Z SCT110. OTLK...VFR.
PLAINS
  NRN...OVC060 TOP FL180. VIS 3SM SN BR. 18Z OVC070. VIS 3-5SM
    SCT -SHSN. OTLK...MVFR CIG SN BR.
  SRN...OVC080 TOP FL180. WDLY SCT -SHSN. 18Z ISOL -SHSN.
    OTLK...MVFR CIG SHSN.

.
AZ
NRN...SKC OR SCT CI. OTLK...VFR.
SRN...BKN CI. OTLK...VFR.

.
NM
NWRN...SKC. 19Z SCT CI. WND W G25KT. OTLK...VFR.
SWRN...SKC. 16Z SCT CI. OTLK...VFR.
NERN...OVC070 TOP FL180. 19Z SKC. OTLK...VFR BECMG 01Z MVFR CIG.
SERN...OVC050 LYRD FL180. VIS 3SM BR. 18Z OVC070. OTLK...MVFR CIG BR.

WINDS ALOFT

```
FT  3000   6000  9000   12000  18000  24000  30000  34000  39000
PHX 2505 2810+06 3012+00 3117-04 2921-17 3025-31 293346 282956 293860
PRC        3011+01 3115-05 3121-18 3031-32 303347 293756 303461
TUS    2906+05 3015+01 3119-04 3019-17 2926-31 283246 273156 284459
```

Radar

RADAR

✦(Radio Detection And Ranging)

How RADAR works

✦2 Types:

- *Primary Radar*
- *Ground based (No airborne equipment required)*
- *Transmits narrow radio waves by a rotating beacon*
- *When the radio waves strike a/c, the waves are reflected back to the antenna*
  - These waves are seen as echoes
- *Line of sight is required*
- *Distance of aircraft is determined by amount of time waves take to come back*
- *No actions required by pilots*
- *No additional equipment needed*
- *Azimuth or angle of a/c is also measured*
- *Problems with Primary:*
  - Temperature inversions can bend radio waves making them less accurate
  - Ground obstacles (mtns, bldgs) can clutter return
  - Precipitation can produce a return
  - Overshadowing (aircraft hidden in precipitation or behind other a/c)
  - Size of target (small targets may not reflect enough energy to produce a return e.g. B747 vs. C172)
- *Secondary Radar*
- *Developed to overcome shortfalls of primary*
- *Signal is sent out from the ground (interrogator signal)*
- *Transponder inside a/c picks up signal, boosts it and sends it back w/ stronger signal (transponder reply)*
- *Line of sight*
- *Advantages:*
  - Specifically ID aircraft (squawk codes)
  - Not as degraded by weather
  - Equally displays different size aircraft
  - Provides altitude info
- *Disadvantages:*
  - Relies on pilot participation
  - If no mode C, no altitude info
  - Requires additional equip.

Radar Environment

✦Radar services
- *Traffic alerts*
- *Vectors*
  - Can help if get lost
  - Can give altitudes based on MVA(Minimum Vectoring Altitude)
    - Controllers have access MVA
- *Ground Speed indications*
- *Can Help you Locate a fix*

✦ATC (Air Traffic Control)
- *Tower*

✦ARTCC (Air Route Traffic Control Center)
- *Usually deal with traffic above 10,000'MSL*
  - Workload permitting, can provide services below
- *20 centers across US*
  - Used to monitor a/c en route flight
  - Found in A/FD, charts

✦TRACON (Terminal Radar Approach Control)
- *Provide Radar Services in airport vicinity*
- *Usually in B and C airspace*
- *Resembles B and C airspace grey marker line*

Surveillance Radar

- *ARSR- Air Route Surveillance Radar*
  - Long range
  - Used by ARTCC for en-route flights
  - Usually over 10,000'
  - If workload permits, under 10,000'
    - VFR flight following
  - Found in AF/D
- *ASR- Airport Surveillance Radar*
  - Short range
  - Airport environment

Radar Vectoring

✦Procedure used by ATC to steer pilot by giving specific heading
✦Once a controller gives vectors, they assume obstacle clearance
✦Aircraft doesn't need NAV equipment to be vectored
✦Terminology

- *"Radar Contact"*
  - aircraft has been identified and will receive radar services
- *"Radar Contact Lost"*
- *they lost contact*
  - Make position reports
- *"Radar Services Terminated"*
  - pilot will no longer receive radar services
- *"Resume Own Navigation"*
  - end of radar vectors, pilot in charge of navigation

✦Uses
- *Departure- helps get established on course*
- *En-route- traffic separation or sequence, weather advisories*
- *Arrival- helps get established on final approach course*
  - Vector before final approach fix (FAF) within 30° intercept
  - ATC should inform pilot if being vectored across approach course
  - Maintain last assigned heading and altitude until given further clearance

Radar Approaches
✦Airport Surveillance Radar Approach
- *Non-precision*

✦Precision Approach Radar
- *Precision*

Surveillance Approaches (SAR)
✦Non precision approach executed by ATC giving directions

✦Back-up procedure in case of instrument failure

✦They will give you:
- *Vectors to keep you on course*
- *Descent information*
- *Missed approach point*

✦Uses ASR

✦Example: Ft. Huachuca

Precision Approaches (PAR)
✦Much more accurate because it gives the controller the glide-slope (3°)

✦Requires special radar equipment at the end of each runway

✦ATC will advise

✦When to begin descent

✦The Decision Height

✦When you are at decision height

✦Mostly military (very limited to civilian pilots)

✦Example: Ft. Huachuca

No Gyro Approaches (**AIM 5-4-11)

✦Advise ATC of gyro failure (HSI failure)

✦Declare instrument malfunction (possible emergency) and request a non-gyro approach or GPS approach if GPS is on board. (**FAR 91.187)

✦ATC will assist you by keeping you on the final approach course

- *When to stop and start turns*
  - Standard rate until on final approach course
  - Half standard rate when on final approach course

✦Pilot still responsible for vertical descent because it is understood that the NAV equipment is still working

✦Airport must have ASR or PAR to support request

✦ATC may provide the following: (They are not required to proved these services)

- *Discrete frequency*
- *Vectors*
- *Advise when to descend*
- *Altitude and distance from runway*
- *Missed approach point*
- *Each mile along approach course*

Transponder Operations

✦Function selections

- *Off*
- *On*
- *ALT- transmits pressure altitude*
- *STBY- on but not transmitting- used for warm up*
- *TEST- used to make sure unit is working and to test pressure altitude (sends reply)*

✦IDENT button

- *Causes transponder to send a signal to highlight the contact on the radar screen*

✦Code selector

- *Can be set to display numbers 0-7*
- *4096 codes are possible*
- *1200 VFR*
- *7500 Hijack*
- *7600 lost comm.*
- *7700 emergency*

✦Mode A-
- *no altitude- old style, not in use anymore*

✦Mode C-
- *altitude, most common*

✦Mode S-
- *alt, tail number, type aircraft, weather info, ATC clearance*
- *Reduces workload for controllers*
- *Might become the "new mode C"*

DME

DME
✦(Distance Measuring Equipment)

How it Works
✦Tells Aircraft
- *Slant range distance in NM to/ from station*
- *Ground speed*
- *ETE to the station*

✦DME Equipment
- *Airborne transceiver*
- *Display*
- *Aircraft antenna*
- *DME ground station*

✦Operation
- *Always paired with a Navaid*
- *Aircraft transceiver sends out a signal, and ground station responds with a ranging reply*
- *Distance determined by time of signal to go and come back*
  - Distance = Time x Speed
- *With time, DME can determine GS and distance to station and ETE*
  - ETE and GS only accurate if flying directly TO the station
- *DME has range of 199 NM*
  - Line of sight
- *Responds to 100 strongest signals (can handle up to 100 a/c at a time)*
- *Identify by Morse code*
  - Same as Navaid it's paired with
  - VOR is transmitted every 10 seconds
  - DME is a higher pitch and transmitted every 30 seconds
- *Must positively ID before using/navigating*

✦Errors
- *Slant range distance (draw picture) (GPS in R22 does not have this error)*
- *Distance is calculated and includes your altitude*
  - The error can be 3% of distance or .5 NM, whichever is greater
- *The higher and closer you are to DME, the greater the error*
- *Prevention- Stay below 1000' per 1 NM*
- *Groundspeed only accurate when flying directly to the station*

DME Frequencies

✦Operates on frequency of 962-1213MHz (UHF)

✦252 frequencies available

VOR/DME Pairing

✦When paired, the frequencies are paired together

- *By tuning VOR, the DME is automatically tuned in as well*

✦DME is sometimes paired with VOR's

- *Can determine direction from station and distance*

ILS/DME Pairing

✦DME is sometimes paired with ILS

✦The DME station is located close to the rwy. threshold

- *Provides "distance to go" to the runway threshold*

DME Arcs

✦Circular flight path centered on ground station or navaid

✦Protected airspace of a published DME arc is ± 4NM (Jackson Hole)

✦Used to:

- *Align aircraft with final approach path or a departure procedure*
- *Change radials*
- *Obstacle Clearance*

✦To perform:

- *At ½ mile(depends on speed) prior to desired DME, turn 90° in direction of radial we want to intercept*

✦Twist 10°, turn 10° when CDI is at or below OBS

✦Must remain within 1 NM of DME assignment

✦Show example from approach plate (Yuma) (Colorado)

✦e.g.. Inbound on R-360 to TFD. Fly at 10 DME Arc to intercept R-330 to proceed inbound.

VOR

VOR

✦(Very high frequency Omni-directional Range) (PPM 9-21)

Principles of Operation

✦Equipment sends 2 signals that our a/c intercepts and follows to

✦Variable Phase

- *Signal is varied slightly for each degree*
- *Signal sent out in one direction but rotating at 1,800 RPM (Lighthouse beacon)*

✦Reference Phase

- *Same signal omni-directionally*
- *Signal emitted in all directions when variable phase is at 360° creating radials (Strobe above lighthouse)*

✦Contains Morse code identifier broadcasted every 10 seconds

- *3 cod identifier = normal operation*
- *4 code identifier = testing*

Ground Station

✦Transmits radials outward in every direction. There is 1 radial for every degree. (Spokes on a bicycle wheel) (Fig. 9-17)

VOR/DME and VORTAC

✦Provide distance and course guidance

✦Frequencies 108.00 MHz to 117.95 MHz

✦Line of sight which limits use at lower altitudes

✦Accurate within one degree

Airborne Equipment and Cockpit Display

✦Antenna, receiver and an indicator

✦Indicator consists of:

- *OBS (Omni-Bearing Selector)-*
  - Twist knob to select desired radial and/or center needle
- *CDI (Course Deviation Indicator)-*
  - Needle to show how **FAR off the radial a/c is or isn't
    - Needle deviates left or right to show relation of aircraft to course
    - CDI deflection scale marked in dots
    - Each dot is 2°
    - Up to 10° (5 dots), after that it will still indicate 10°
    - Distance from course = 200ft(constant)x(number of dots)x(N.M.)
  - TO/FROM indicator-

• Tells us if we're going to/from the station

VOR's Displayed on Aeronautical Charts

✦Charts show

- *Frequency, position and Morse code identifier*

✦Magnetic north arrowhead usually on compass rose

✦Compass rose marked every 30°

✦Victor Airways

- *Marked on either end of the radial out of the VOR*

VOR Course Navigation

✦Allows for navigation by using VOR to remain on course

- *VOR to VOR*
- *VOR to Fix*
- *Fix to Fix along a radial*

✦Plan routes using VORs

VOR Navigating

✦Tune to freq. and identify station w/Morse code

✦Must ID station before using it

- *If no signal, check frequency. If correct: DO NOT use*
- *Test signal indicated by: (-....-)*

✦Determine radial by:

- *Twisting OBS until needle centers and indicates TO*
- *You can determine position by using 2 VORs (Show on chart)*
- *On charts, intersections are labeled with 5 letter names*

✦Select radial by:

- *Twisting OBS to desired radial and flying towards the needle*

✦Always fly to the station w/TO flag and from w/FROM flag

VOR Cautions

✦Cone or Zone of confusion (Draw picture)(PMIF 268)

- *Lack of signal directly above the station*
- *Flight over top of VOR*
- *Flag may go away*
- *Continue to fly magnetic heading*

✦Reverse sensing (Set needle to desired radial)

Classes of VORs (**AIM 1-1-8)

✦Terminal VOR

- *-25 NM below 12,000' AGL*

- Guaranteed Signal
- ✦Low Altitude VOR
  - *-40 NM between 1,000 – 18,000' AGL*
    - Guaranteed Signal
- ✦High Altitude VOR (most common)
  - *-40 NM up to 14,500' AGL*
  - *-100 NM 14,500 – 18,000' AGL*
  - *-130 NM 18,000 – 45,000' AGL*
  - *-100 NM 45,000 – 60,000' AGL*
    - Guaranteed Signal
- ✦*For altitudes below 1,000' AGL, refer to **AIM 1-1-9 (p. 524- 2011 version)

Types of VORs
- ✦VOR = VHF VOR
  - *Civil use*
- ✦VOR/DME civil use
  - *VOR paired with DME on same frequency*
- ✦TACAN = Tactical Air Navigation-VOR & DME
  - *Military use*
  - *Requires special equipment for VOR*
  - *Civilians can use DME*
- ✦VORTAC = VOR & TACAN
  - *Both military and civil use*
  - *Both VOR and DME*

RMI (Radio Magnetic Indicator)
- ✦Also in Lesson Attitude Instrument Flying
- ✦Combines the functions of HI and MC
- ✦Magnetic Flux Valve
  - *senses magnetic direction and sends electrical signals to the HI to align it with the magnetic heading of the aircraft (Known as Slaving)*
    - Flux Valve is under floorboard PIC
- ✦Slaving meter indicates differences HI and Mag. Heading
  - *Left deflection indicates counterclockwise error*
    - Press left button in the free gyro mode
  - *Right deflection indicates clockwise error*
    - Press right button

HSI (Horizontal Situation Indicator)
- ✦A remote indicating compass with VOR/ILS navigation indications

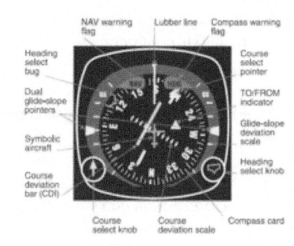

- ✦5 components
  - *Flux valve*
  - *Slaving unit*
  - *Gyro(under passenger seat)*
  - *Nav/Com*
  - *Display*
- ✦Additional Features
  - *VOR and Localizer info*
  - *Glide-slope*
  - *No Reverse Sensing tracking to VOR (With HSI)*
    - Reverse Sensing can happen when flying back course of localizer
      - Fly the tail of OBS to avoid on BC (Instrument Flying p.292) (TUS)
      - Fly the head of OBS to avoid on front course

VOR Intercepting and Tracking
- ✦Tune and ID station
  - *Select course with OBS*
  - *Track To or From station*
- ✦Intercept Angles
  - *90° intercept expedites radial intercept while sacrificing tracking towards station*
  - *60° intercept equalizes track and intercept*
  - *30° intercept allows more of a course travel than intercept (Use as per QH unless a good reason not)*
- ✦Figuring Time and Distance Without DME
  - *Turn 90°*
  - *Time how long it takes to go 10° or 10 radials*
  - *Turn inbound*
    - Minutes x 60 = Time to Station
      - Radial Change
    - Minutes x TAS = Distance to Station
      - Radial Change

VOR Instrument Approach (91.171)
- ✦Use approach plate and explain
- ✦VOR receiver check
  - *Required by regulations*
  - *If VOR is used under IFR, it must be checked every 30 days*
  - *Requires a log entry in logbook or any other record (SPED)*

- Signature
- Place of check
- Error
- Date
- *Types (VODGA)*
  - VOT(vor test facility)
    - Found in AF/D
    - Test VOR that sends out 360 radial in all directions
    - 360 from or 180 to
    - (+/-) 4°
  - Owner/operator
    - Fly along a victor airway
    - Select ground reference on a victor airway at least 20 NM away from VOR
    - Center CDI, note radial
    - Airborne check +/- 6°
  - Dual VOR
    - Tune both to same radial
    - Within 4°of each other
  - Ground checkpoint
    - Found in AF/D
    - Specific position on airport
    - Tune and select specific radial +/- 4 degree error
  - Airborne checks
    - Found in AF/D
    - Specific altitude, distance, radial, fly over reference point
    - Center CDI, note radial
    - +/- 6°
- ✦Preferred Order of Checks: VGAOD (FAA Approved)

NDB/ADF

NDB

- ✦(Non-Directional Beacon)
  - *Ground based transmitter sends radio signal in all directions*
  - *Low-med frequency 200-1750 kHz (AM)*
  - *Morse code identifier*
  - *Not restricted to Line of Sight*
  - *Works like compass needle and points to station*
    - Needle is accurate within 2°
- ✦NDB Classes
  - *Compass locator - 15NM Range*
    - -NDB integrated with Outer or Middle marker of ILS system (LOM)
  - *MH (medium high) -*
    - 25NM
  - *High (H) -*
    - 50NM
  - *High High (HH) -*
    - 75NM
- ✦NDB Limitations (CMINT)
  - *Coastal Effect*
    - Signal bends slightly towards coastline when crossing at <30°
    - Must fly perpendicular to coast by 30° or more
  - *Mountain Effect*
    - Signal reflects off mountains
  - *Interference*
    - Other NDBs interfering with similar freqs.
    - AM radio stations can also interfere with signal
  - *Night Effect*
    - Signal refracted or bent by ionosphere
      - A part of the upper atmosphere
    - Results in wandering needle
  - *Thunderstorm Effect*
    - Needle deflects toward lightning

ADF

- ✦(Automatic Direction Finder)
- ✦3 Components

- *ADF Receiver*
  - Installed in cockpit on instrument panel
  - Pilot tunes to desired NDB and verifies w/ID
  - Must monitor and identify Morse code using receiver
- *2 Antennas (PPM Fig. 9-33)*
  - Loop Antenna
    - Rotating sensor narrows the signal to two possible directions
    - Normally mounted on bottom of aircraft
    - Imagine a tunnel
  - Sense Antenna
    - Determines which direction signal is coming form based on signal strength.

Cockpit Display

✦Bearing
- *Horizontal direction from one point to another*

✦Magnetic heading
- *Direction helicopters pointed*

✦Relative bearing (Draw)
- *Difference between the aircrafts heading and the straight line drawn from the aircraft to the station*

✦Magnetic bearing
- *Magnetic heading to the station*
- *MH + RB = MB (Mike Had Roast Beef Mike Barfed)*

✦3 types of bearing indicators:
- *Fixed Bearing Indicator (PPM Fig. 9-37)*
  - 0° always appears at the top
  - Numbers around 360° card correspond to a station relative to the nose of the aircraft
  - To fly directly to a station:
    - Must add MH+RB=MB
    - If total is more than 360 subtract 360 to find (MB)
    - Ex. MH 330 + RB 060 = MB 030
- *Rotatable Card Bearing Indicator*
  - Rotatable card has to be manually aligned with aircraft heading
- *Radio Magnetic Indicator (RMI) (slaved)*
  - Similar to moveable card except it automatically adjusts to present aircraft heading (Gyro)
  - Has flux Valve

Station Identification

✦Station identification
- *3 letter Morse code*
- *Pilot must continually monitor Morse code*
  - Display doesn't have NAV flag

Orientation

✦Needle points to the station
- *Can determine direction to/from station*
- *Where you are (In relation to the station)*
- *Where you want to go*
- *How to get there*

✦Must be used with another instrument to be accurate when outbound
- *HSI*
- *Compass*

Intercepting/Tracking/Navigation

✦Intercept less than 90° angle
✦2 types of navigating
- *Homing*
  - Flying towards without wind correction angle
  - Flying the needle(curved flight path)
- *Tracking*
  - Applying a wind correction angle to fly a direct course
  - **AIM for a precise WCA using bracketing of 10 degrees

RMI/DME Arcs **PMIF

✦Just prior to desired distance, turn 90 degrees in the desired direction
✦Needle should be at the wingtip
- *Let it get 10° behind*
- *Turn 20° ahead and let needle get 10 degrees behind and repeat until just prior to reaching desired radial*
  - 5° for 10NM DME is more accurate

GPS

GPS (PMIF 341)

Global Positioning System
✦Maintained by DOD
- *Satellite based*
  - 21 operational and 3 spares
    - 6 Paths
      - 12 hour orbits
  - 5 are always in view of user
    - Need 4 to determine 3-D position
    - Need 3 for two dimensional position
  - Continually broadcasts signals
    - Receiver calculates position

✦3 Elements
- *Satellites*
- *Receiver*
- *DOD controlled*

✦Receiver
- *Antenna pick up signals*
- *Needs 4 satellite signals*
- *Information from receiver*
  - GS
  - Position
  - ETA
  - Distance from
  - Distance off desired track
    - Linear deviation- unlike VOR which is angular
  - Altitude
- *Can be displayed on HSI*

✦Advantages
- *Can perform non-precision approaches anywhere*
  - Hospitals, Oil rigs
- *Not Line of Sight*
- *Unaffected by weather*
- *No need to fly over ground based navaids*

✦Disadvantages
- *Must have satellites in view to be accurate*

- *Terrain shadows (flying through valleys)*
- *Aircraft shadowing*
- *Signal Interference from radios*
- *Selective availability-Department of Defense can degrade the accuracy of signal*
- *Note:*
- *Do not rely on vertical navigation from GPS unless it has WAAS (Wide Area Augmentation System) or LAAS*

✦Sensitivity
- *Lateral not angular (Explain)*
- *3 Phases*
  - En route
    - More than 30NM from waypoint
    - Full deflection=5NM
  - Terminal
    - 30NM to 2NM from FAF
    - Full scale=1NM
  - Approach
    - Within 2NM of FAF to Missed Approach Point
    - Full Scale=0.3NM
- *RAIM-receiver autonomous Integrity Monitoring*
  - Need a minimum of 5 satellites or 4 if receiver has baro-aiding
  - Approach must be loaded in to GPS
  - GPS approach requires R**AIM check by FAF
    - Done by assuring GPS is in Approach mode (APR)
    - Goes into APR 2 miles before FAF (This is where we get R**AIM)
      - If no APR by FAF or lost on approach, STOP descent, go to MAP and execute missed approach procedure.
- *INTEG-integrity mode*
  - Lets you know the GPS is not working properly
  - Any phase of flight

Regulations
✦Cannot be the only means of navigation, alternate NAVAID needed
- *If RAIM, monitoring of alternate NAV isn't required*

✦To be approved for IFR, must have an up-dateable database

✦Handheld GPS not authorized for IFR flight
- *Situational awareness only*

✦GPS for IFR flight must comply with Technical Standard Order

- *(TSO)129a, AIRBORNE SUPPLEMENTAL NAVIGATION EQUIPMENT USING THE GLOBAL POSITIONING SYSTEM (GPS)*

✦Must be update every 28 days to be used in IFR

GPS Substitutions

✦DME, including the requirement above 24,000 ft.

✦DME ARC

✦Navigating to or from NDB

- *NDB holding, course*

RNAV

✦(Area Navigation)

✦Creates artificial VORs(waypoints) using signals from real VORs

- *Allows for straight flights not over the VORs*

✦Same concept as GPS, but uses VOR not satellite

✦Needs signal from VOR in order to work

✦Linear deviation unlike angular from VOR

SIDs and Approaches

✦Must have at least two waypoints

- *Waypoints must be defined by both:*
  - Latitude and Longitude
  - Radial and distance from a VOR

LORAN

✦(Long Range Navigation)

✦Transmitting stations arranged in a chain (AM frequency)

- *Master station transmits pulse*
- *Secondary transmits after master*
- *Computer determines a Line of Position (LOP)*
  - Need 2 LOP to determine position

VHF DF

✦(Direction Finding, DF Steer)

✦Special antenna at ground based ATC facility that can detect the direction of VHF-COM signals

- *Voice communication*
- *Simply pushing the microphone will allow VHF DF ability*

✦Directional information is displayed to a controller on a radar screen, then the controller can advise the pilot with a heading to fly

✦Controller can determine a fix with readings from 2 or more DF stations

◆No special airborne equipment is needed
◆Mainly used in emergency situations—lost procedures

Precision Approaches
✦Provide horizontal and vertical guidance

✦More accurate with lower descent altitudes

✦3 Types:
- *ILS - Instrument Landing System*
- *PAR - Precision Approach Radar*
- *MLS - Microwave Landing System*

INSTRUMENT LANDING SYSTEM (ILS)

✦4 components of ILS
- *(Casa Grande ILS RWY 5) (**AIM 1-1-9)*
- *Localizer-*
  - Horizontal guidance
- *Glide-slope-*
  - Vertical Guidance
- *Marker Beacons-*
  - Situational Awareness
- *Approach Lighting System (ALS)-*
  - Situational Awareness and guidance

Localizer
✦Frequency 108.10-111.95 MHz(VHF)
- *Odd tenths frequencies*
- *Forty frequencies available*
- *Morse code identifier*
  - Four letters, always starts with I (Show example on chart)

✦Antenna at end of rwy. sends out 2 signals (Instrument Flying pg. 291, Fig. 13-4)(Draw)
- *150hz(VHF) (Blue Lobe)*
- *90hz(VHF) (Yellow Lobe)*

✦Course width (Instrument Flying pg. 292, Fig. 13-5)
- *Signal is 700' wide at threshold of runway*
- *3-6° wide, average is 5°*

✦Localizer CDI sensitivity
- *4X more sensitive than VOR*
- *Each dot = .5°*
- *Full scale deflection = 2.5°*
- *Course width = 5°*

✦Range of localizer
- *35° wide from centerline of threshold up to 10NM away*
- *10° wide from centerline of threshold up to 18NM away*

✦Back Course (Instrument Flying pg. 292, Fig. 13-7)
- *LOC transmits signal behind and creates BC*
- *Non precision approach, no glideslope*
- *When flying back course, set the OBS to front course heading and fly the tail of OBS to avoid reverse sensing*
- *Published LOC Back Course approach plate (TUS)*

✦Flying the localizer
- *ID and confirm functionality*
- *Align CDI with final approach heading*
- *Keep CDI centered*
- *Make small corrections*
  - No bigger than the width of the heading bug

Glideslope

✦Vertical guidance to TDZ
- *Usually set at 3°*
- *Usually a loss of altitude by about 300 ft. per NM*

✦Similar to a localizer, but it is on it's side (Instrument Flying pg. 299, Fig. 13-16)
- *90hz top(UHF) (Yellow Lobe)*
- *150hz(UHF) (Blue Lobe)*

✦Transmitter location
- *750-1250' from the threshold **IFH*
- *400-600' from the centerline **IFH*
- *Offset in order to give more than one aircraft glide slopes*

✦Range of 10NM

✦False glide slope at 12.5° (Instrument Flying pg. 300, Fig. 13-17)
- *To avoid, always intercept from below*
- *Sensitivity of vertical CDI*
- *12X more sensitive than VOR and 3X more than localizer*
- *.35° per dot: HSI*
- *Width = 1.4° from top to bottom*
- *Full scale deflection = .7°*
- *35' x # of dots x # of Nautical Miles*
  - 2 dot deflection:
    - = 70 ft. at 1 NM

- = 140 ft. at 2 NM
- = 210 ft. at 3 NM.
- = 350 ft. at 5 NM.
- = 700 ft. at 10 NM.

✦Flying the glideslope
  - *Intercept glideslope around FAF*
  - *Use appropriate speed to stay on glideslope*
    - Use small corrections
    - Approach angle may be noted on approach plate
    - Descent rate equal to 5 times the groundspeed
      - -A/S X 5 = rate
      - -80KTS GS X 5=400' min rate of descent
  - *Final Approach Point (Not FIX) is the glideslope intercept*
  - *MAP is at Decision Height(DH) (AGL) or Decision Altitude(DA) (MSL)*
  - *At DH/DA:*
    - Power, Pitch, Talk, switch back to VOR

Marker Beacons **PMIF
✦Provide range fix on approach
✦Help with situational awareness
✦3 types of marker beacons:
  - *Outer marker(OM)*
    - 4-7 nautical miles out on approach
    - About 1400'AGL
    - Blue light, continuous beep (------), low pitch
    - Usually positioned around the point the pilot should intercept the glideslope
  - *Middle marker(MM)*
    - 3500' from runway
    - About 200'AGL
    - Amber light, six beeps per second (-.-.-.), medium pitch
    - Aircraft is close to D.A. or D.H.
  - *Inner marker(IM)*
    - Usually on category II or III approaches (**FAR 1.1)
    - 100' agl
    - White light, 95 dots/dashes per minute (......), high pitch
✦Marker beacons can be replaced by
  - *Outer marker by VOR*
    - DME fixes

- *NDB paired with a marker beacon is called a compass locator*
  - LOM
    - Outer compass locator
    - NDB paired with OM
  - LMM
    - Middle compass locator
    - NDB paired with MM

ALS (Approach Lighting System) (**AIM pg 563)

✦ALS extends out 2400'-3000' on a precision approach
  - *1400'-1500' on non-precision*

✦REIL (Runway End Identifier Lights)
  - *White strobe lights at end of runway*

✦RAIL (Runway Alignment Indicator Lights)
  - *Extended centerline of runway*
  - *Sequenced flashing lights*

Other Airport Lighting

✦VASI (Visual Approach Slope Indicator) (Instrument Flying pg. 309)
  - *2 Bar*
  - *3 Bar*
  - *Tricolor*
  - *PVASI- Flashing/ Pulsating*

✦PAPI (Precision Approach Path Indicator) (Instrument Flying pg. 309)
  - *4 lights in a row*

✦VASI and PAPI Indications: (PMIF 309-10)
  - *White over white, high as a kite*
  - *Red over white, you're alright*
  - *Red over red, you're dead*

✦Runway Lights
  - *Different Intensities*
  - *7 HIRL (High Intensity Runway Lights) 7 clicks*
    - 5 MIRL (Medium Intensity Runway Lights) 5 clicks
    - 3 LIRL (Low Intensity Runway Lights) 3 clicks
  - *Touchdown Zone Lights (green)*
  - *Taxiway Lights*
    - Centerline is green
    - Edge is blue

Precision Instrument Runway Markings (**AIM 2-3-1, 2-3-2, 2-3-3)

✦Threshold markings

✦Touchdown zone (500')

✦**AIMing point (1,000')

✦Fixed distance markers (first 1,000')

Inoperative Components

✦Localizer out

- *cannot fly approach.*

✦Glideslope out

- *turns into localizer only. (higher minimums/ non-precision)*
- *Vertical guidance done by step-sown altitudes on IAP*

✦Marker beacons out

- *Doesn't change approach unless MB req. for approach.*

✦ALS out

- *visibility requirements (possibly)go up as stated on approach plate.*

Simultaneous Approaches (PMIF 321)

✦Airport must have a minimum of 4,300' between runways

Parallel Approach

✦Minimum of 2,500' between runways

✦Stagger aircraft by 2 miles

Converging Approach

✦MAP(missed approach point) must be 3 miles apart

✦MAP must be going in different directions

Sidestep Maneuver

✦Used to sidestep to parallel runway

- *Using normal maneuvers*

✦Runway must be closer than 1,200'

✦Pilot must have visual of both runways

OTHER ILS TYPE APPROACHES

Localizer Type Directional Aid (LDA)

✦Comparable to a localizer but isn't aligned with runway

- *If significantly misaligned, it will not be assigned a number*

✦Can have glideslope, but it is never a precision approach

✦If final course is greater than 30° from runway heading = circling minimums only

✦If final course is less than 30° = straight in and circling minimums

Simplified Directional Facility (SDF)

✦Course width is either 6° or 12°

✦Never has a glide slope

✦May or may not be down centerline of runway (offset)

✦Aligned within 3° of runway

Microwave Landing System (MLS)

✦Precision approach

✦Curved microwaves

• *Curved flight path*

✦Special airborne equipment required

Wind Shear on Approach

✦Come in shallow and fast keeping ETL for as long as possible

✦Undershoot effect: IAS drops, you must increase power to keep from descending

✦Overshoot effect: IAS increases; you must decrease power to slow airspeed and keep from climbing

Holding

Holding Procedures
✦A "race track" like pattern typically on approach but also en-route
✦Reasons for holding
  - *Sequencing of a/c for landing*
  - *Spacing from other a/c*
  - *Allowing WX to clear*
  - *Lose altitude*
  - *Procedure turn or missed approach*
✦5 Elements of a Hold (show on IAP)
  - *The holding fix*
  - *The holding radial or bearing*
  - *The position of the holding pattern relative to the fix*
  - *The direction of turns*
  - *The timing*

Published Holds
✦Denoted on approach plates
✦Elements of published holds:
  - *Same as non-published but displayed in picture form*

Standard Holding Pattern
✦Right turns
✦1 min. inbound leg

Tracking in a Holding Pattern
✦Inbound leg is always main tracking leg
✦Inbound leg is always toward the holding fix

Wind Correction
✦Headwind or Tailwind (Show Handout)
  - *Plan for a 1 minute inbound*
  - *Adjust outbound to achieve 1 minute inbound*
    - If inbound is 1:15 then subtract :15 from outbound leg :45 to achieve a 1 minute inbound leg on next inbound leg
✦Crosswinds
  - *Determine wind correction angle on your inbound leg*
  - *Use 10° wind correction angle for your outbound leg, not to exceed 30° (draw holding pattern and crosswind)*

- If a steep turn is needed, then wind is blowing us into holding pattern
- If shallow turn is needed, then wind is blowing us out of holding pattern
  - Once inbound WCA is determined, double it for outbound.

Entry of a Hold
✦Used to determine the most efficient way to enter a hold (Show Handout)

✦Thumb Technique
- *Set heading bug on outbound heading*
- *Determine direction of turns*
  - Use right thumb for right turns, left for left turns
- *3 Types*
  - Direct
    - cross over fix (5 T's)
    - standard rate turn to outbound heading
    - fly level for 1 minute
    - Standard rate turn in proper direction 180 ° toward inbound
    - intercept inbound
  - Teardrop
    - cross holding fix
    - turn 30° toward the top for correction for outbound course
      - right turns, subtract 30°
      - left turns, add 30°
    - fly 1 minute
    - Standard rate turn in proper direction 180 ° toward inbound
    - intercept inbound
  - Parallel
    - cross fix
    - turn to outbound heading
    - fly 1 minute(parallel inbound)
    - turn 180° in opposite direction of pattern turns and intercept inbound
    - track inbound
- *5T's*
  - Turn
  - Time
  - Twist
  - Throttle
  - Talk

Non-Published Holds

✦Issued by ATC and you're given 5 minutes prior to the hold fix (**AIM 5-3-7)

✦Elements of non-published holds:

- *Fix*
- *Radial or bearing (NDB)*
- *Direction of turns (If no direction given, assume Right Turns)*
- *Position of hold from fix (N, S, E, W, NE, NW, SE, SW)*
- *Timing (Typically 1 minute, above 14,500'- 1.5 min is standard)*
- *EFC (Expect Further Clearance)*
  - Do NOT accept a hold without and EFC

Non-Standard Holding Pattern

✦Everything else (e.g. Left turns, 2 min. inbound leg)

Procedure Turns

✦Maneuver for course reversal to get lined up on final approach course

✦Typically used to facilitate positioning for final approach course

✦Indicated by a thick black line (missed approach procedures are thin line)

✦4 Types:

- *Racetrack (most common)(CGZ VOR 5)*
  - holding pattern layout
  - holding entries to determine course reversal
  - mandatory if in bold
- *45/180 (IWA ILS & VOR 30C)*
  - turn 45° for 1 minute
  - turn 180° to intercept final approach course
  - not mandatory
  - 5NM limitation for helicopters (IFH 8-18, **AIM 5-4-9)
- *80/260*
  - turn 80°
  - immediately turn 260° in opposite direction to intercept
  - 5NM limitation for helicopters (IFH 8-18, **AIM 5-4-9)
  - not mandatory
- *Base turn/ teardrop*
  - track outbound on a radial for a specific time/distance
  - followed by a turn to intercept inbound
  - rare but mandatory when published as depicted

✦PT's Mandatory Unless:

- NoPT on approach plate
- Timed approaches from a holding fix

- Radar vectors
- If not approved by ATC

DME ARCS

✦A curved maneuver flown at a specific distance from the DME ground facility.

✦Usually flown as a series of short straight legs, rather than a steady curve.

✦Often used to transition from en route phase to an intermediate approach segment or final approach course of an instrument approach.

✦Establish a 90° intercept angle to the DME arc using heading bug

✦At about ½ mile distance from the arc, turn 90° to intercept

✦Twist the OBS 10° and then turn 10° to stay on the desired arc.

Holding Pattern With No Wind

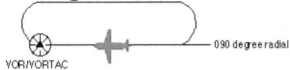

VOR/VORTAC
VOR/VORTAC holding. The VOR/VORTAC is the Fix.

Holding Pattern With A Headwind

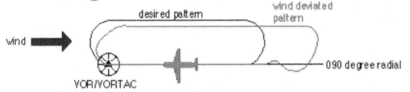

Headwind Time on Inbound leg:
    Inbound: 1 minute
    Outbound: Shorter
Tailwind Time on inbound leg:
    Inbound: 1 minute
    Outbound: Longer

Holding Pattern With A Crosswind

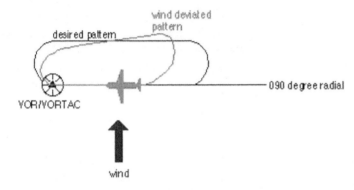

Examples:
Hold east on 10 DME Radial 235
Hold south of 10 DME on Radial 180 of IWA VOR EFC 10 min

IFR Regulations

**FAR PART 1 DEFINITIONS AND ABBREVIATIONS

✦If the student has a question about what a term means or is looking for clarification, this is a good source. Also review the important ones with student.

**FAR PART 61 CERTIFICATION: PILOTS, FLIGHT INSTRUCTORS, AND GROUND INSTRUCTORS

61.3 PIC under IFR flight plan or in IMC

✦Pilot must hold current instrument rating

- *Must have an instrument rating to enter Class A (91.135)*

✦Must present certificate for inspection if requested by:

- *the administrator,*
- *An authorized NTSB representative,*
- *federal, state or local law enforcement, or*
- *An authorized Representative from the TSA (Transportation security administration)*
- *Which includes Instructors from Flight Schools*

61.19 Duration of pilot and instructor certifications

✦Discuss if needed

61.51 Pilot Logbooks (g)

✦Pilot may log as instrument time only that time aircraft is flown solely by reference to instruments

- *Can be actual or simulated*

✦CFII can only log instrument time when in IMC

✦Logging time for recent experience, must include

- *Location of approach*
- *Type of approach*
- *Safety pilot name (If needed)*

61.57 Recent Flight Experience (a) (c) (d)

✦To carry passengers within preceding 90 days:

- *Day*
  - Performed 3 takeoffs/landings of same category, class, type
  - Sole manipulator of flight controls
- *Night*
  - Performed 3 takeoffs/landings of same category, class, type
  - Sole manipulator of flight controls
  - 1 hour after sunset/1 hour before sunrise

◆Instrument experience
- *Must be actual or simulated IMC*
- *Within preceding 6 calendar months*
  - 6 instrument approaches
  - Holding procedures
  - Intercepting and tracking courses through the use of NAVAID systems
- *If not completed with the preceding 6 months the pilot then has 6 months after that to accomplish these requirements before they must do an IPC*

◆Instrument proficiency check
- *Alternative way to regain or maintain instrument currency*
- *Qualifies pilot as IFR current for next 6 months*
- *Only valid for the category of aircraft involved*
- *Can be taken at any time*
  - Not required if current by other means
- *Must be given by*
  - FAA examiner
  - FAA designated examiner
  - Any CFII
  - Company check pilot
  - Military check pilot (Only applies to military pilots)
- *Tested in*
  - Appropriate aircraft
  - Use tasks and limitations out of **PTS

61.65 Instrument Rating Requirement
◆Part 61 only (reference only)

FAR PART 91 GENERAL OPERATING AND FLIGHT RULES

91.3 Responsibility of the Pilot in Command
91.21 Portable Electronic devices
91.103 Pre-flight action (FADWAR)
◆F-fuel requirements

◆A-alternates

◆D-delays

◆W-weather

◆A-aircraft performance

◆R- runway lengths

91.109b Flight instruction in simulated conditions

91.123 Compliance with ATC clearances and instructions
91.131 Operations in Class B
✦IFR Operation
- *Operable VOR or TACAN receiver is required*
- *Mode C transponder required*
- *Two-way radio required*

91.167 Fuel Requirements for IFR
✦Complete flight to first airport of intended landing or
✦Fly from first airport of intended landing and then to an alternate airport
- *And fly after that for 30 minutes at normal cruise speed*

✦An alternate (#2 above) is not necessary if destination airport has an instrument approach, and:
- *Weather minimums exist at ETA plus 1 hour of:*
  - Ceiling 1000' above elevation of airport or 400' above lowest applicable approach minimum, whichever is highest
  - Visibility is greater than 2 statute miles

91.169 IFR Flight Plan (a,2 b, ii, c)
✦Filing
- *Information required same as VFR flight plans (§91.153(a))*
- *File a minimum of 30 minutes prior to ETD*
- *FSS will hold flight plan for one hour (**AIM 5-1-13) after ETD;*
- *Prescott FSS will hold flight plan for 2 hours*

✦Alternate Airports
- *No alternate required if*
  - At estimated time of arrival (ETA) to 1 hour after
    - Ceiling 1000' above airport elevation
      - OR (whichever is highest)
      - 400' above lowest applicable approach minimum
    - AND
    - 2 SM visibility
- *If weather is less than above, then an alternate is required:*
  - Alternate with instrument approach
    - If alternate has an instrument approach you must look on the airport diagram of the approach plates and see if that approach is approved to use as an alternate
    - At ETA
      - Ceiling must be 200' above minimums for approach flown
      - AND

- 1 SM visibility but not less than minimum for approach flown
  - Alternate without instrument approach
    - Ceiling and visibility must allow descent from MEA in basicVFR conditions to airport
- ✦Cancellation of flight plan
  - *PIC can call FSS, ATC Facility, or ARTCC before or after landing at an airport without tower*
  - *Automatically cancelled if at a towered airport and flight is complete*

91.171 VOR Equipment Check (VODGA)
✦Operations check every 30 days
- *VOT—180 TO or 360 FROM*
  - *±4°*
- *Operator (own)*
  - Select a known location on a radial (at least 20 n.m. away from VOR)
  - *+6°*
- *Dual Check (need 2 VOR receivers)*
  - Center both needles; must read within 4° of each other
- *Ground Check*
  - Found in AF/D (is a ground location at an airport; will tell you where to be and what radial to tune to
  - *+4°*
- *Airborne Check*
  - Found in AF/D (airborne location, usually over a prominent ground landmark)
  - A visual checkpoint to fly over and a specific radial to tune into the VOR
  - *+6°*

✦Record in aircraft logbook (SPED)
- *Signature*
- *Place of check*
- *Amount of bearing Error*
- *Date*

91.173 ATC Clearances and Flight Plan Required
✦No person may operate under IFR unless
- *Filed flight plan (IFR)*
- *Received appropriate ATC clearance*

91.175 Takeoff and Landing under IFR
✦Takeoffs
- *No minimums for Part 91*

- *Pilot should use approach minimum in case of emergency landing (make sure that you could come back and land)*

✦Landings
- *Use published instrument approach procedure minimum for that airport*
- *In order to descend below DH or MDA*
  - Perform normal maneuvers and landing (Part 121 or 135 in TDZN)
  - Visibility not less than prescribed minimums
  - At least one of the following criteria must be met:
    - ALS is in sight
      - you may descend below MDA/DA to 100' above touchdown zone until
        - The red terminating bars, red side row bars or one of the airport environment visual references are visible and identifiable.
        - If no ALS, you cannot descend below DH or MDA until one of the airport environment visual references are visible and identifiable.
    - An Airport Environment Visual Reference is in sight
      - AEVR's include:
        - Threshold
        - Threshold Marker
        - Threshold Lights
        - Touchdown Zone
        - Touchdown Zone Marker
        - Touchdown Zone Lights
        - Runway
        - Runway Marker
        - Runway Lights
        - REIL
        - VASI

✦Missed Approach
- *Immediately execute missed approach if any one of the following conditions occur:*
  - At DH and you do not have visual contact with the airport environment
  - If sight is lost after descending below DH or MDA
  - Upon reaching DME MAP and at MDH
  - Limitation on procedure turns
- *Pilots are not allowed to make procedure turns when:*
  - Being vectored on final approach course or fix
  - Timed approach from holding fix
  - No procedure turn if (NoPT) published
  - No pilot may make a procedure turn unless ATC has cleared them to do so

✦ILS Components
- *(GLAM)*
  - Glideslope
  - Localizer
  - Approach light system (ALS)
  - Marker beacons

91.177 Minimum Altitudes for IFR

✦No aircraft may operate below
- *MEA or MOCA*
  - Only may operate below MEA if MOCA is a lower altitude
- *In areas where no minimum altitude is prescribed*
  - Mountainous areas (**AIM 5-6-5)
    - -2000' above highest obstacle within 4 NM
  - Other areas
    - -1000' above highest obstacle within 4 NM

✦Climbs
- *Begin immediately after passing point for which higher altitude was prescribed*
- *Or climb as appropriate to achieve the MCA*

91.179 IFR Cruising Altitudes (WEEO)

✦In controlled airspace
- *Maintain altitude assigned by ATC*

✦In uncontrolled airspace (<18k WEEO) (Not WEEO + 500)
- *Magnetic heading 0—179—fly odd thousands*
- *Magnetic heading 180-359—fly even thousands*

91.181 Course to be Flown

✦Unless authorized by ATC
- *Must fly federal airway along the centerline*
- *On another route—must fly directly between fixes*

✦In VFR conditions aircraft is allowed to maneuver to avoid other aircraft

91.183 IFR Radio Communication

✦PIC of A/C under IFR must cont. monitor appropriate freq. and shall report:
- *In radar contact: (MARVELOUS)* **AIM 5-3-3
  - Missed approach
  - Altitude changes
  - Reaching a clearance limit / hold
  - VFR on top altitude change

- Estimated true A/S changes +/ 10kts or 5% whichever is higher
- Leaving a clearance limit or fix
- Outage of NAV or COMM equipment (7600)
- Unable to climb / descend 500fpm
- Safety of flight
- *Not in radar contact: (MARVELOUS)+(LEP) **AIM 5-3-3*
  - Leaving FAF or outer marker
  - Estimated arrival time change of +/- 3min
  - Position reports
    - Position reports: (dark triangle) (IPTATEN) **AIM 5-3-2
      - ID of aircraft (7193U)
      - Position (over TFD VOR)
      - Time in zulu
      - Altitude/flight level
      - Type of flight plan
      - ETA and name of next reporting point
      - Name only of following point

91.185 IFR Two-Way Radio Communications Failure

✦VFR (squawk 7600)

- *Maintain VFR and land as soon as practical*
  - If VFR conditions during IFR flight after radio failure, remain in VFR

✦IFR (squawk 7600)

- *Route (in order)(AVE-F)*
  - last Assigned
  - If being Vectored, direct from point of failure, to fix
  - The route ATC told you to Expect
  - as Filed
- *Altitude (use highest of the following per each segment of route)(MEA)*
  - Mea
  - Expected altitude
  - Last Assigned
- *Clearance Limit (a point in space that you cannot go beyond without receiving an additional clearance)*
  - Can be one of two things
    - Point from which the approach begins
      - w/ EFC
        - Fly to the fix where approach begins
        - Hold until EFC

- Shoot approach
  - w/o EFC
    - Fly to the fix where approach begins
    - Hold until ETA
    - Shoot Approach
- Point that is not where approach begins
  - w/ EFC
    - Fly to clearance limit
    - Hold until EFC
    - Continue to the fix where approach begins
    - Hold until ETA
    - Shoot approach
  - w/o EFC
    - Fly to the fix where the approach begins
    - Hold until ETA
    - Shoot approach

91.187 Malfunction reports
✦As Soon As Practical, report to ATC
- *Aircraft ID*
- *Equipment that failed*
- *Degree of importance*
- *Level of support or assistance requested*

91.203 Required Inspections
✦A1late
- *Annual*
- *100 hour inspection*
- *Life Limited Parts*
- *Airworthiness Directives*
- *Transponder*
- *Emergency Locator Transmitter*

91.205 Equipment Requirements (d)
✦All instruments and equipment required for VFR day and night
- *Review*

✦Instruments for IFR
- *GGGICARA*

✦DME above FL240 when using VOR for navigation

✦Mode C above 10,000

✦VOR in Bravo

91.211 Supplemental Oxygen

✦Flight Crew

- *At or below 12,500' MSL*
  - No oxygen required
- *Between 12,500' MSL - 14,000' MSL*
  - 30 minute max without oxygen (crew)
- *Above 14,000' MSL*
  - Oxygen required at all times (crew)
- *Above 15,000' MSL*
  - Passengers must be provided with O2

91.411 Altimeter System & Altitude Reporting Tests

✦For flight under IFR

- *Within preceding 24 calendar months*
  - Pitot static system
  - Altimeter
  - Automatic pressure reporting system must have been tested and inspected
- *No person may operate a helicopter in controlled airspace under IFR unless these inspections are completed*

91.413 ATC Transponder Tests

✦No person may use transponder unless:

- *Within the preceding 24 calendar months it has been tested and complies with part 43*

✦TAPE-V (IFR Instrument Inspections)

- *Transponder*   *24 mos*
- *Altimeter*   *24 mos*
- *Pitot-static system* *24 mos*
- *ELT*   *12 mos*
- *VOR*   *30 days*

**FAR PART 95- IFR ALTITUDES*

✦See also **AIM end of chapter 5 for additional reading

**FAR PART 97- STANDARD INSTRUMENT APPROACH PROCEDURES (SIAP) (TERP)*

97.1 Applicability
97.3 Symbols and terms used in procedures

49 CFR NTSB PART 830

Incident and Accident Reporting

✦Accident

- *occurs between the time of boarding and disembarkation of an aircraft with the intention of flight which results in:*
  - Death (WITHIN 30 DAYS)
  - Serious injury
    - Requires hospitalization for more than 48 hours
    - Starting within 7 days of when injury was received
    - Fracture of any bone
    - Except simple fractures of fingers, toes or nose
    - Severe hemorrhages, nerve damage, muscle or tissue damage
    - Internal organ damage
    - Second or third degree burns affecting more than 5% of the body surface
    - Aircraft receives substantial damage

✦Incident

- *Occurrence other than an accident associated with the operation of aircraft or safety of operation*

Immediate Notification to the NTSB (830.5)

✦Accidents

- *Written report must be submitted within 10 days*

✦Overdue aircraft

- *Written report must be submitted after seven days if aircraft is still missing*

✦Incidents listed below: (FACTFOIDH)

- *Fire in Flight*
- *Aircraft Collision*
- *Crew unable to perform duties due to illness or injury*
- *Turbine component failure*
- *Failure of flight controls*
- *Overdue aircraft presumed down*
- *12,500 pound aircraft*
- *Damage to property exceeding $25,000*
- *Helicopter tail rotor or main rotor damage*

Information to be given w/ written report (830.6)
Must be given for an incident when requested (830.10)

✦Preservation of Aircraft involved in accident

- *Operator is responsible for preserving any wreckage, mail, cargo and records*
- *Prior to NTSB taking custody of wreckage, don't move anything unless:*

- To remove persons injured or trapped
- To protect wreckage from further damage
- To protect public from injury

• *If moving of wreckage is necessary, make sketches, take notes or photos of original positions of moved objects*

• *Operator of aircraft must retain all records, reports, internal documents and memos until authorized by board*

✦Reports and Statements to be filed

- *Accidents*
  - Within 10 days
- *Incidents*
  - Whenever requested by representative of board
- *Overdue aircraft*
  - After 7 days if still missing

**AIM CHAPTER 10*

Table 10-1-1
**AIM 10-1-2

✦Helicopter use of standard instrument approach procedures

• *1. Helicopters may reduce the visibility minima by 1/2 but no less than 1/4 statute mile visibility or 1200 RVR.*

10-1-3 All

✦Helicopter Approach Procedures to VFR airports

- *Approach to Specific Landing Site*
  - Approach is aligned within 30° of landing rwy.
  - Pilot must maintain visual contact with landing site at or prior to MAP
  - Must maintain published viz. throughout the visual segment
  - Upon reaching MAP, advise ATC whether proceeding visually and canceling IFR or complying with MAP instructions
  - At least one of the following visual references must be visible or identifiable before the pilot me proceed visually:
    - FATO or FATO lights
    - TLOF or TLOF lights
    - Heliport instrument lighting system
    - Heliport approached lighting system
    - Visual glideslope indicator
    - Wind sock or windsock light
    - Heliport beacon

- Other facilities or systems approved
- *PinS (Point in Space Approaches)*
  - MAP is located more than 2 SM from landing site
  - Required turns greater than 30°
  - Visual contact w/ landing site is not required however you must maintain the higher of VFR WX minimums
  - Upon reaching MAP, advise ATC whether proceeding visually and canceling IFR or complying with MAP instructions

IFR Flight Planning

IFR FLIGHT PLANNING

Preflight Considerations

✦Pilot qualifications
- *Instrument rated*
- *Current*

✦IMSAFE

✦Aircraft IFR equipped

✦Weather
- *Departure*
- *Arrival*
- *Alternate if required*

✦NOTAMs

✦Charts/plates/sectionals
- *SIDS*
- *En route charts*
- *STARS*
- *SIAP's*
- *Sectionals*

✦Flight logs complete and accurate

✦Fuel Logs accurate with reserve

✦IFR flight plan filed

✦FADWAR

En-Route Charts

✦Airport information
- *Voice communication panel*
- *Elevations*

✦Navigational Aids
- *VORs and VORTAC*
  - Basis for Airways
  - HIWAS and TWEB

✦Routes
- *Federal Airways*
  - Controlled airspace
  - 18,000-1200AGL victor airway
  - Above 18,000 called Jet routes

- Info about airways
  - Mag. Course
  - Distance
  - MEA or MOCA

Route to Fly

✦MEA- Minimum En route Altitude
- *Nav coverage and obstacle clearance between fixes*
- *2000' for mountainous terrain and 1000' non-mountainous*

✦MOCA- Minimum Obstruction Clearance Altitude
- *Red T following number*
- *Obstacle clearance and nav coverage (22NM from station)*

✦MCA- Minimum Crossing Altitude
- *Minimum safe altitude to cross over a point on a defined route*

✦MRA- Minimum Reception Altitude
- *Min altitude to ensure reception from VOR*
- *Determines an intersection*

✦COP's - Change over Points
- *Change from one VOR to another*
- *If no COP published, change over at halfway point or whenever there is a bend in the route*

✦MORA-Minimum Off route Altitude
- *2000' clearance*

✦MAA-Maximum Authorized Altitude
- *Highest usable altitude ensuring NAV coverage*

Airports

✦Approaches available
- *Missed approach procedures*

✦Find all runway lengths and widths in A/FD or IAP chart

✦Draw a diagram of runways and ramps for reference as well as any obstacles for landing or take-off

✦Field elevations

✦Applicable minimums

✦Circling runways available and obstacles around this maneuver

✦Runway approach lighting available

✦Any pertinent information necessary for safe flight

Navigation Aids

◆Depicted on charts along with relevant frequencies and identifiers

◆Show various navigation facilities on en-route chart.

Routes

◆Plan Route (**FAR 91.181)

- *Draw a line from departure to destination or choose the appropriate victor airways*
- *Using the IFR plotter, draw a straight line from the departure point to the destination point*
- *Responsible for own obstacle clearance and navaid reception when using a direct routing.*
- *Mountainous regions- 2,000 feet from obstacle*
- *Non-mountainous regions- 1,000 feet from obstacle*
- *Avoid MOA's, Prohibited Airspace, or Restricted airspace if it cannot be entered*
  - ATC will vector you on new airways if your filed flight plan involves flight in an active MOA

◆Measure distance (be sure to use the appropriate scale on the IFR plotter)

◆Set up checkpoints

- *Find and note compulsory reporting points*
- *Make change-over points (COP's) checkpoints on your flight planning*

Airspace

◆Review Class A,B,C,D,E,G

- *Dimensions*
- *Requirements to enter*
- *Clouds and Visibility*

Communications

◆FSS VHF communications frequencies are shown on en route charts near navaid boxes

◆Standard FSS frequency is 122.2

◆Frequencies that can transmit but not receive are labeled with a "G"—guarded

◆You would listen on the VOR frequency and talk on the guarded frequency

◆Emergency frequency—121.5

- *NOT SHOWN ON CHARTS—you must remember this one*

◆RCOs (remote communications outlets)

- *Unmanned communications facilities controlled remotely by ATC*
- *Used to extend communication to pilots operating **FAR away from direct radio coverage*

◆CTAF frequencies are also found on en route charts for uncontrolled airports

- *Also found on SIDs and SIAPs*

◆Determine all necessary frequencies

- *ATIS*

- *Clearance Delivery*
- *Ground*
- *Tower*
- *Departure*
- *Flight Service Station*
- *Unicom*
- *Approach*
- *TWEB, AWOS, etc.*
- *Emergency (121.5)*

Flight Planning

✦Route selection

- *Preferred IFR Route*
  - Established route ATC would prefer you to fly to help traffic flow during certain times of the day.
  - Found in AF/D
- *Tower Enroute Control Routes(TEC)*
  - Allows IFR flight by communicating through towers instead of ARTCC
  - Found in AF/d page 353
  - Short flights (less than 10,000' and 2 hours)
- *Off-airway navigation*
  - GPS or RNAV
  - Plan altitudes with at least 1000' clearance
- *Availability of SIDS and STARS*
- *Altitude Selection*
  - Use IFR altitudes
  - WEEO (NOT +500')
  - At or above MEA
- *Weather Briefing (1800-WX-BRIEF) or www.duats.com*
- *NOTAMS*

✦Alternates

- *No alternate required if*
  - At estimated time of arrival (ETA) to 1 hour after
  - Ceiling 1000' above airport elevation
    - OR (whichever is highest)
  - 400' above lowest applicable approach minimum
  - 2 SM visibility
- *If weather is less than above, then an alternate is required:*
  - Alternate with instrument approach

- If alternate has an instrument approach you must look on the airport diagram of the approach plates and see if that approach is approved to use as an alternate
- At ETA Ceiling must be 200' above minimums for approach flown
- AND
- 1 SM visibility but not less than minimum for approach flown
- Alternate without instrument approach
  - Ceiling and visibility must allow descent from MEA in basicVFR conditions to airport

✦Communication and Navigation information
- *Determine nav. and comm. frequencies*
  - Show where to find and where to put
- *Compute A/S, time, fuel*
  - Show student how
- *Fill out flight plan and file 30 minutes prior to departure*
  - Composite flight Plan
    - 1st portion VFR
      - Open VFR flight plan after departure
      - While in VFR, close VFR flight plan and request IFR clearance
    - 1st portion IFR
      - Normally cleared to point of change
      - As you approach clearance limit, If in VFR, cancel IFR, Open VFR
      - If still in IFR, request further clearance from ATC
- *Other considerations*
  - Delays
  - Runway lengths
  - Weight and Balance
  - Vne
  - Position reporting points (Mandatory and not)

Conclusion
A complete understanding of how and why we flight plan. More specifically how to plan an IFR flight and the differences from VFR.

Revised IFR Flight Planning
1. Obtain WX for planned route
✦Current, Forecasted, Winds Aloft, Hourly Forecast, NOTAMS, etc...
- *Determine whether or not an alternate is required (91.161)*
✦Fill in Aircraft number, Dep, Dest, and Date on Nav. Log
2. Select route and waypoints using Low En-route Chart

✦Determine if there are any SID's at dep. airport and use if published

✦Use obstacle departures if one published for airport

✦If no obstacle departure, use standard departure procedures (See Handout)

✦When departing apt. not on a Victor airway, you must fly directly to nav. aid, or waypoint.(VOR, or intersection) (91.181)

✦When not on a Victor airway, plan route(4NM on each side) and altitude for the specific route as follows: (See VFR charts)

- *Mountainous- 2,000 ft. above highest obstacle (91.177)*
- *Non-mountainous- 1,000 ft. above highest obstacle (91.177)*

✦Determine if there are any STAR's at dest. Airport and use if published

✦Determine best published approach to use

3. Identify Nav. frequencies and identifiers
4. Identify Comm. frequencies for route

✦Emergency- 121.5

✦Flt. Watch- 122.0, 122.2, 122.4, 122.6

5. Determine course to each checkpoint

✦Radials/Headings

6. Determine distance to each checkpoint
7. Determine appropriate altitudes for the route

✦Consider MEA's along route

✦Consider MOCA's along route

- *May descent below MEA but not below MOCA (91.177)*

✦Consider altitudes for approach flown

8. Determine magnetic course for each segment
9. Perform weight and balance

✦Consider fuel requirements for IFR (91.167)

✦Interpolate winds and temps. for required altitudes

✦Temps may not be std. lapse rate. Calculate change per altitude.

✦Convert winds to magnetic north.

10. Calculate performance and limitations

✦Temp, Vne, MAP, IAS, CAS, TAS

11. Calculate data for each segment with flight computer

✦TAS = Airspeed>Plan TAS

✦Course and GS = Plan Leg>Hdg/GS

✦Leg Time = Plan Leg>Leg Time

✦Fuel Burn = Fuel>Fuel Burn

✦Calculate Top of Climb in first leg calculations

12. Calculate other considerations (FADWAR) (91.103)

✦Elev, Temp, Weight, OGE, IGE, Rwy. Lengths

IFR Departures

CHECK WEATHER AT DEPARTURE AIRPORT

✦ATIS

✦AWOS

✦ASOS

✦Rotating beacon operating in daylight indicates visibility <3SM and ceiling less than 1000'AGL (IFR conditions)

TAKEOFF MINIMUMS

✦(Published on back/front of airport diagram)

✦Apply to commercial traffic if published

- *Part 91 pilots do not have to comply with minimums (**FAR p. 179 [f])*
  - Not a good idea to takeoff if less than approach minimums for departure airport

✦3 Ways To Depart an Airport

- *SID (Standard Instrument Departure) (Published)(Show example)*
  - Published route to transition from terminal to an en-route structure
    - Simplifies issuance of departure clearance at busy airports
    - Controller provides name of SID instead of more complex clearance
  - To accept a DP (SID), pilot must have at least a textual description in the cockpit
  - If you do not want to accept a SID, put "No SID" in remarks section of flight plan
- *ODP (Obstacle Departure Procedure) (Published on airport diagram)*
  - May require greater climb rate or a flight path to follow (e.g.. CHD)
- *Standard Takeoff Procedures (Handout)*
  - Standard 200'/NM, climb at least 400' AGL before turns
  - Calculated by: (# of ft./NM x G/S) ÷ 60 [e.g.. 200 x 60 ÷ 60]

✦RVR (Runway Visual Range)

- *Visibility down runway in feet*
  - Measured with a transmissometer

SETTING UP AIRCRAFT FOR DEPARTURE

✦Before takeoff

- *Departure control freq.*
- *Transponder code*
- *Local Altimeter Setting*
- *Set up VOR receiver and OBS if being used for navigation.*

✦Standard 200'/NM, climb at least 400' AGL before turns

✦Continue climbing to MEA at best rate of climb

ATC Clearance

✦File flight plan 30 min prior

✦Contact clearance delivery/ground before starting engine for clearance (CRAFT)

- *Obtain clearance not more than 10 minutes prior to proposed taxi time*

✦C.R.A.F.T. (See below for examples)

- *Clearance Limit*
- *Route*
- *Altitude*
- *Frequency*
- *Transponder Code*

✦Clearance Limit: Point to which you are cleared to fly.

- *Examples:*
  - Cleared Tucson International
  - Cleared to Stanfield VORTAC

✦Route: Routing that you are assigned. May not be the same as the one on your flight plan

- *Examples:*
  - R/V to V-105 > TFD > Direct
  - R/V TFD > DINGO FIVE arrival

✦Altitude: Altitude assignment

- *Climb and Maintain: Instruction to climb and fly at that specified altitude*
- *Cleared to Cruise: Instruction to fly, at your discretion, anywhere between the minimum IFR altitude up to and including the altitude in your clearance*
  - No clearance required to climb, but clearance to descent is required
- *Examples:*
  - 3,000 – Expect 5,000 in 3 min
  - 5,000 – Expect 7,000 in 5 min

✦Frequency: Tower will hand you off to departure control

- *Examples:*
  - 123.7
  - 120.7

✦Transponder Code: Discrete code for your aircraft

- *Examples:*
  - Squawk 2131
  - Squawk 4465

✦VOID time

- *If departing from a non-controlled airport, FSS will issue a VOID time*

- Clearance no longer valid if we do not contact ATC by this time
✦Repeat back all information exactly as the controller read it to you (Write it down)
  - *As Filed should be the only time you read back an abbreviated clearance*
  - *Abbreviated clearances will always contain at least the following:*
    - Name of the destination airport or fix (clearance limit)
    - DP and transition, if appropriate
    - Altitude assignment
✦When ready for departure ask for "IFR Release" on the appropriate frequency.

IFR En Route

EN-ROUTE

Radar Service
✦After takeoff, tower will instruct you to change to departure frequency
✦Initial radar ID is "radar contact"
- Radar contact lost= ATC cannot see you on radar
- Radar service terminated= ATC no longer watching you

✦"Resume own navigation"= pilot responsible for navigation
- Radar flight following will continue

En-Route Clearance
✦Read back all numbers and instructions
- *Altitudes*
- *Altitude restrictions*
- *Radar vectors*

✦PIC can accept or refuse clearance
✦Altitude changes should be made without delay

Mandatory ATC Reporting Points (Position Reports)
✦Required when in non-radar environment:
- *IPTATEN*
  - Id
  - Position
  - Time
  - Altitude
  - Type of flight plan
  - ETA and name of next reporting point (Solid triangle or open triangle when required regardless)
  - Name of reporting point to follow

Other Reports
✦When in or out of radar contact, initiate calls when:
- *MARVELOUS*
  - Missed approach
  - Altitude changes (Assigned)
  - Reaching Clearance Limit/entering hold
  - VFR on top altitude changes
  - Estimated true airspeed change of ±5% or 10Kts
  - Whichever is greater

- Leaving a clearance limit or hold
- Outage of communication or navigation equipment
- Unable to climb or descend at 500fpm
- Safety- anything that would affect the safety of flight
  - Any un-forecast weather, malfunctioned gyro, anything unsafe

✦**When NOT in radar contact**
- *Leaving FAF or Outer Marker*
- *ETA changes of 3 minutes or more*
- *Position reports (IPTATEN) + MARVELOUS*
  - ID
  - Position
  - Time (Zulu)
  - Altitude
  - Type of flight plan (VFR, IFR)
  - ETA and name of next fix
  - Name of following fix

Flying Airways
✦Fly centerline
- *Unless passing aircraft in VFR conditions*

✦Protected corridor 8NM wide (4NM on each side of airway)

✦Pilot responsible to see and avoid in VFR even if under radar control

✦Maintain WX awareness
- *EFAS, TWEB,HIWAS*

High Altitude Flying and Oxygen
✦12,500-14,000MSL
- *Pilot and crew must use after 30 min*

✦14,000+
- *Pilot and crew must use all time*

✦15,000+
- *Passengers must be provided with*

VFR on Top
✦Pilot must request

✦Must maintain VFR Wx minimums

✦Fly VFR cruising altitudes (even or odd thousands +500)

✦Stay in VFR conditions

✦Comply with IFR requirements

- *Stay above MEA*
- *Comply with ATC clearances*
- *Make position reports (In radar contact up required- open triangle, Not in radar contact mandatory- closed triangle)*

✦ATC no longer responsible to separate from IFR traffic

✦Not available in Class A

DME Failures

✦Required above FL240 if using VOR

✦Notify ATC immediately and remain at/above FL240 until next intended landing to repair

Enroute Diversions

✦Be familiar with suitable airports along your route

✦Current weather along route

- *ATIS, AWOS, ASOS, EFAS, TWEB*

Minimum Fuel

✦declaring minimum fuel

- *telling atc that you cannot afford any undue delay*
- *not declaring an emergency, just an advisory*

Canceling Flight Plans

✦We don't close IFR flight plans, We "cancel " them

✦Automatically cancelled at controlled airports

✦If VFR conditions exist and we can descend to destination we may cancel

✦Uncontrolled airports

✦Must cancel by phone within 30 min of ETA

IFR Approach

STAR- Standard Terminal Arrival Route

✦Published IFR procedure to transition from en-route to arrival phase/IAF
  * *Simplifies clearance delivery procedures*
✦Can be issued without a request
✦Must have a textual description
✦If you do not want to accept, put "no star" in remarks section
✦Star clearance is not an approach clearance, maintain last assigned altitude

Arrivals

✦Determine how you will get to FAF before departing
✦Check WX en-route to determine if conditions will allow approach
✦Descend promptly when advised
✦When changing from en-route to approach, ATC may advise
  * *Own navigation*
  * *Radar vectors*
  * *Hold*
✦If practice approach in VFR, advise ATC and remain in VFR
  * *Do not fly into clouds when being vectored*

Vertical Navigation

✦Vital during instrument flight
  * *Terrain may not be seen*
  * *Obstacles may not be seen*
  * *Other aircraft may not be seen*
✦Correct altimeter setting is important
  * *Read back to controller when advised to change*

Segments of Instrument Approach (Follow along with example plates)

✦1.) Transition Segment
  * *Also known as feeder routes*
  * *Route from an enroute fix to the IAF*
  * *Course, altitude, distance*
✦2.) Initial approach segment
  * *Starts at IAF*
  * *Maneuvering for approach*

- *Consists of course, radial, dme arc, procedure turn, vectors, holding pattern*

✦3.) Intermediate approach segment
- *Pre landing checks*
- *Positioning and speed adjustments*
- *Ends at FAF*

✦4.) Final approach segment
- *Starts at FAF*
  - Glideslope intercept for precision
  - Maltese Cross for non precision (specific altitude)
- *May be straight in or circling approach*
  - Circling if approach is not aligned with runway
- *Alignment and descent for landing*
- *Timing is commenced at FAF to assist with MAP determination*
- *Pilot must not descend below MDA or DA until visual contact made with airport (**AIM 5-4-21)*

✦5.) Missed approach segment
- *Precision approach MAP= when we reach a certain altitude on glideslope (DA)*
- *Non precision approach MAP= certain distance, time, or facility*
- *Published turns in MAP procedure should not be made until after MAP*
- *If going missed, start climb out immediately to missed altitude but do not turn until MAP*
- *If not Visual then pilot must go missed*
  - Initiate another approach
  - Return to holding pattern
  - Resume flight to diversion point or alternate airport

Instrument Approach Charts (Updated every 56 days)

✦Elements
- *Identification of a particular approach*
- *Full details of radio facilities on the approach*
- *A plan view of the approach and missed approach*
- *A profile view of the approach and missed approach*
  - Holding procedures associated with the approach
  - Necessary airport and topographical information pertinent to safe flight
  - Minimum Safe Altitude (MSA) circle (25NM unless specified)

✦Approach minimums for helicopters
- *½ of published for planes but not less than ¼ SM*
- *Timing to the missed approach point*

Factors of minimums

◆Type of approach

◆Equipment on aircraft

◆Approach light system

◆Obstacles

◆Approach speed (Helicopters are category A on NACO charts)

◆Straight in versus Circling

Visual Reference at DH or MDA (**FAR 91.175)

◆Review.

Visual Descent Point (V)

◆A point that commercial operations use to maintain a certain approach angle.

◆At this point, if you have the req. visual references, you can descend below MDA.

Minimum Safe Altitudes (MSA)

◆1000' altitude clearance

◆Usually 25 NM coverage from facility

Helicopter Approaches (**AIM 10-1-3)

◆Approach to Specific Landing Site

- *Approach is aligned within 30° of landing rwy.*
- *Pilot must maintain visual contact with landing site at or prior to MAP*
- *Must maintain published viz. throughout the visual segment*
- *Upon reaching MAP, advise ATC whether proceeding visually and canceling IFR or complying with MAP instructions*

PinS (Point in Space Approaches)

◆MAP is located more than 2 SM from landing site

◆Required turns greater than 30°

◆Visual contact w/ landing site is not required however you must maintain the higher of VFR WX minimums or what's published on approach plate.

◆Upon reaching MAP, advise ATC whether proceeding visually and canceling IFR or complying with MAP instructions

Landing Illusions

◆Wider runways, Down-sloping causes high approach

◆Narrow runways, up-sloping causes low approach

◆Fog, haze, rain causes low approach

Visual Maneuvering
✦Circle to Land
- *If not within 30° of runway*
- *Visual maneuver to land*
- *Usually done when making landing on runway other than the one approached*

Visual Circling Maneuver
✦Maintain MDA or higher until able to begin descent

✦Wind direction and speed determining factor for runway

✦Should be as close to normal pattern as possible

✦Descent below MDA should not be made until
- *Visual reference with the airport environment is established*
- *The landing threshold is in sight*
- *The required obstacle clearance can be maintained on the approach*

Circling Area
✦Based on Speed

✦Category A covers 1.3 N.M. of the airport environment

✦Highest obstacle + 300' is MDA

Sectored Circling Areas (Instrument Flying p. 575)
✦Excludes extra high obstacle(e.g.. Circle to land NA south of the runway)
- *Gives lower MDA*

Missed Approach When Circling
✦Anytime lose visual, execute missed approach

✦Make any turns toward the runway

✦Advise ATC of missed

Circling Minimums Only:
✦Will be published if
- *Runway is more than 30° out of alignment with the final approach path, or*
- *Descent gradient from FAF to the runway is excessive—requiring a high rate of descent for a straight in landing*

Airports Without IAP
✦Alternate needs to be filed

✦Can make approach to nearby airport and then proceed VFR

✦Can descend to MEA/MOCA and cancel IFR if in VFR and proceed to airport

Contact Approaches

◆Used in lieu of published approach

◆Pilot has to request, ATC cannot assign

◆Pilot responsible for obstacles and traffic

◆Airport must have instrument approach procedure

◆Must be on an IFR flight plan

◆Conditions:
- *1 SM visibility*
- *Clear of clouds*
- *Expectations that conditions won't change*
- *Visual of airport in not required*

Visual Approaches

◆ATC can assign, or pilot can request

◆Eases ATC workload

◆Prior to accepting,
- *VFR conditions (1,000' ceiling, 3 SM viz.)*
- *Clear of clouds*
- *Airport or preceding aircraft in sight*
- *Still on IFR flight plan*
- *Still responsible for obstacles and traffic*

Visual Illusions

◆Wider runways, Down-sloping causes high approach

◆Narrow runways, up-sloping causes low approach

◆Fog, haze, rain causes low approach

Wake Turbulence

◆Wingtip vortices
- *Greatest are aircraft*
  - Heavy, slow, and clean configuration

◆Stay above flight path of larger aircraft when taking off or landing

◆Most dangerous with a quartering tailwind

CPSIA information can be obtained
at www.ICGtesting.com
Printed in the USA
LVOW03s0315031215

465121LV00012B/108/P